INTRODUCTORY LEVEL Six-Way Paragraphs

100 Passages for Developing
the Six Essential Categories of Comprehension

THIRD EDITION

WALTER PAUK

JAMESTOWN PUBLISHERS

a division of NTC/CONTEMPORARY PUBLISHING GROUP
Lincolnwood, Illinois USA

Readability

Passages 1–25: Level A

Passages 26–50: Level B

Passages 51–75: Level C

Passages 76–100: Level D

ISBN (introductory level): 0-8442-2124-4
ISBN (middle level): 0-8442-2119-8
ISBN (advanced level): 0-8442-2123-6

Published by Jamestown Publishers,
a division of NTC/Contemporary Publishing Group, Inc.,
4255 West Touhy Avenue,
Lincolnwood (Chicago), Illinois 60712-1975 U.S.A.
© 2000 by NTC/Contemporary Publishing Group, Inc.
Manufactured in the United States of America.

4 5 6 7 8 9 10 11 12 113 09 08 07 06 05 04 03 02

Contents

The Paragraph

The paragraph! That's the working unit of both writer and reader. The writer works hard to put meaning into the paragraph; the reader works hard to take meaning out of it. Though they work at opposite tasks, the work of each is closely related. Actually, to understand better the job of the reader, one must first understand better the job of the writer. So, let us look briefly at the writer's job.

One Main Idea. To make their meaning clear, writers know that they must follow certain basic principles. First, they know that they must develop only one main idea per paragraph. This principle is so important that they know it backward too. They know that they must not try to develop two main ideas in the same paragraph.

The Topic Sentence. The next important principle they know is that each main idea can be stated in a topic sentence, and that such a sentence best serves its function by coming at or near the beginning of its paragraph. They know too, that the more clearly they can state the topic of a paragraph in the opening sentence, the more effective they will be in developing a meaningful, well-organized paragraph.

One word of warning to the reader: There is no guarantee that the topic sentence will always be the first sentence of a paragraph. Occasionally, a writer will start off with an introductory or a transitional sentence. Then, it is up to the reader to spot such a sentence and recognize it for what it is.

The topic sentence may be placed in several other positions in a paragraph. It may be placed in the middle, or even at the very end. If it appears at the end, though it may still be a topic sentence in form, in terms of function, it is more rightfully a *restatement*. Whenever the end position is chosen, it is chosen to give the restatement especial emphasis.

Finally, a paragraph may not have a topic sentence in it at all. Some writers purposely leave out such sentences. But, in such cases, inferring a topic sentence may not be as difficult as it may first appear. Here's why. Many such professional writers actually do write topic sentences, but on separate scraps of paper. They then place one of the scraps at the head of a sheet and use the topic sentence to guide their thoughts in the construction of the paragraph. With the paragraph written and the topic sentence having served its purpose, the scrap is discarded. The end result is a paragraph without a visible topic sentence, but the paragraph, nonetheless, has embedded in it all the clues that an alert reader needs for making an accurate inference.

Finding Meaning. Actually, there is nothing especially important in recognizing or inferring a topic sentence for its own sake. The important thing is that the reader use the topic sentence as a quick means of establishing a focal point around which to cluster the meanings of the subsequent words and sentences that he or she reads. Here's the double-edged sword again: just as writers use topic sentences to provide focus and structure for presenting their meaning, so the perceptive reader can use the topic sentence for focus and structure to gain meaning.

Up to this point, the reader, having looked secretly over the writer's shoulder, should have learned two exceedingly valuable secrets: first, expect only one main idea in each paragraph; and secondly, use the topic sentence to discover the topic of each paragraph.

Supporting the Main Idea. Now, there is more to a writer's job than writing paragraphs that consist of only bare topic sentences and main ideas. The balance of the job deals with developing each main idea through the use of supporting material that amplifies and clarifies the main idea and, many times, makes it more vivid and memorable.

To support their main ideas, writers may use a variety of forms. One of the most common is the example. Examples help to illustrate the main idea. Other supporting materials are anecdotes, incidents, jokes, allusions, comparisons, contrasts, analogies, definitions, exceptions, logic, and so forth.

To summarize, the reader should have learned from the writer that a textbook-type paragraph usually contains these three elements: a topic sentence, a main idea, and supporting material. Knowing this, the reader should use the topic sentence to find the main idea. Everything other than the main idea is supporting material used to illustrate, amplify, and qualify the main idea. So the reader must be able to separate the main idea from the supporting material, yet see the relationship between them.

To the Student

The Six Types of Questions

In this book, the basic skills necessary for reading factual material are taught through the use of the following six types of questions: subject matter, main idea, supporting details, conclusion, clarifying devices, and vocabulary in context questions.

Subject Matter. This question looks easy and often is easy. But don't let that fool you into thinking it isn't important. The subject matter question can help you with the most important skill of all reading and learning: concentration. With it, you comprehend and learn. Without it, you fail.

Here is the secret for gaining concentration: After reading the first few lines of something, ask yourself, "What is the subject matter of this passage?" Instantly, you will be thinking about the passage. You will be concentrating. If you don't ask this question, your eyes will move across the lines of print, yet your mind will be thinking of other things.

By asking this question as you read each passage in this book, you will master the skill so well that it will carry over to everything you read.

Let's see how this method works. Here is a short passage:

> The owl cannot move its eyes. The eyes are fixed in their sockets by strong muscles. But to make up for this drawback, nature gave the owl a special kind of neck. This neck allows the owl to turn its head in almost a full circle. It can do this without moving the rest of its body.

On finishing the first sentence your thought should have been something like, "Ah, a passage about the owl. Perhaps I'll learn some secret of the wise old bird." If it was, your head was in the right place. By focusing right away on the subject matter, you'll be concentrating, you'll be looking for something, your attitude will be superb, and best of all, you'll be understanding, learning, and remembering.

Main Idea. In reading anything, once you have grasped the subject matter, ask yourself, "What point is the writer trying to make?" Once you ask this question, your mind will be looking for an answer, and chances are that you will find one. But if you don't focus in this way, all things seem equal. Nothing stands out.

Try to find the main idea in the following passage by asking, "What point is the writer trying to make?"

> As an orange tree gets older, its fruit improves. Young trees bear fruit that has a thick rind and many seeds. As the tree becomes older, however,

the skins become thinner and the fruit becomes much juicier. The seeds decrease in number. Some old, neglected trees bear fruit with a thin skin and luscious flavor. Some orange trees growing in the Azores bear fruit until they are 100 years old. They produce a highly prized fruit that is thin skinned, full of juice, and free from seeds.

A good answer is, "As an orange tree gets older its fruit gets better." This passage is fairly easy to figure out because the first sentence is an excellent topic sentence.

The next example does not have a topic sentence. Nevertheless, the question "What point is the writer trying to make?" can still be answered. This time, think about the passage and come up with your own answer.

Did you ever wonder how much salt is contained in seawater? Here's a simple experiment you might want to try. Take a can six inches deep. Fill it with seawater. Allow the water to evaporate. There will be about two inches of salt left in the bottom of the can. Just think, if all the seawater on the earth evaporated, it would leave a layer of salt about 230 feet thick!

This passage may have required a bit more thought, for the correct answer is a summary type answer. Compare your answer with the following main idea statement: "Seawater has a large amount of salt in it."

Supporting Details. In common usage, the word *detail* has taken on the unrespected meaning of "something relatively unimportant." But details are important. Details are the plaster, board, and brick of a building, while main ideas are the large, strong steel or wooden beams. A solid, well-written passage must contain both.

The bulk of a factual passage is made up of details that support the main idea. The main idea is often buried among the details. You have to dig to distinguish between them. Here are some characteristics that can help you see the difference between supporting details and main ideas.

First, supporting details come in various forms, such as examples, explanations, descriptions, definitions, comparisons, contrasts, exceptions, analogies, similes, and metaphors.

Second, these various kinds of details are used to support the main idea. The words themselves, supporting details, spell out their job. So when you have trouble finding the main idea, take a passage apart sentence by sentence, asking, "Does this sentence support something, or is this the thing being supported?" In other words, you must not only separate the two, but also see how they help one another. The main idea can often be expressed in a single sentence. But a sentence cannot tell a complete story. The writer must use additional sentences to give you the full picture.

The following passage shows how important details are for providing a full picture of what the writer had in mind.

> Many of the first houses in America were made of bricks taken from ships. Ships, of course, weren't made of brick, but they often carried bricks as ballast. Ballast is heavy material put in the bottom of ships to keep them steady in the water. If a ship is heavier on the top than on the bottom, it is in trouble. The ship will tip over. Many of the ships that came to this country when it was young were almost empty except for bricks and sailors. The sailors knew that they could fill their empty ships with goods from the New World. When the ships arrived in America, their bricks were unloaded and sold. The sailors then had room to put goods from America in the ships' holds in place of the bricks.

Here we have the main idea in one sentence—the first sentence. Having stated the main idea, the writer goes on to explain why the bricks were used in ships and how they ended up being used to build houses. All of the sentences that tell us this information are giving us supporting details.

Conclusion. Some passages contain conclusions. Others do not. It all depends on the writer's purpose. For example, some passages describe a process—how something is done. There is no sense in trying to draw a conclusion from such a passage.

There are two kinds of passages with conclusions. In one, the conclusion is stated by the author. In the other, the conclusion is merely implied by the author. That is, the author seems to have come to a conclusion, but has not stated it. It is up to you to draw that conclusion.

Look for the conclusion that is stated in the following passage.

> The Earth's atmosphere cuts off all but about 47 percent of the sun's radiation. This is enough to warm our planet but not enough to make it boiling hot. The same heat keeps the earth warm after sunset. The warmth is trapped in the atmosphere, which acts like a blanket to keep us warm. It helps to keep temperatures from falling off too quickly after dark.

The author's conclusion is that the Earth's atmosphere acts like a blanket to keep the planet warm.

In the next excerpt, the author strongly implies a conclusion, but does not state it directly.

> The great enemy of the earthworm is the mole. The pewit bird knows this. In order to make the worms think that a mole is near, the pewit taps the ground with one leg. The worms feel a vibration, or shaking motion, in the earth and think it's a mole. They then make their way to the surface to escape. There the pewit waits to snatch its prey.

From the preceding excerpt, we can draw the conclusion that the pewit is an intelligent bird.

Looking for a conclusion puts you in the shoes of a detective. While reading, you have to think, "Where is the writer leading me? What's the conclusion?" And, like a detective, you must try to guess the conclusion, changing the guess as you get more and more information.

Clarifying Devices. Clarifying devices are words, phrases, and techniques that a writer uses to make main ideas, sub-ideas, and supporting details clear and interesting. By knowing some of these clarifying and controlling devices, you will be better able to recognize them in the passages you read. By recognizing them, you will be able to read with greater comprehension and speed.

Two literary devices that make a writer's ideas both clear and interesting are similes and metaphors. Both are used to make comparisons that add color and power to ideas. An example of a simile is "She has a mind like a computer." In this simile, a person's mind is compared to a computer. A simile always uses the words *like, as,* or *than* to make a comparison. The metaphor, on the other hand, makes a direct comparison: "Her mind is a computer." Because metaphors are shorter and more direct, they are more forceful than similes. Writers use them to capture your attention, touch your emotions, and spark your imagination.

The largest single group of clarifying devices, and the most widely used, are transitional or signal words. For example, here are some signal words that you see all the time: *first, second, next, last, finally.* A writer uses such words to keep ideas, steps in a process, or lists in order. Other transitional words include *in brief, in conclusion, above all, therefore, since, because,* and *consequently.*

Organizational patterns are also clarifying devices. One such pattern is the chronological pattern, in which events unfold in the order of time: one thing happens first, then another, and another, and so on. A time pattern orders events. The event may take place in five minutes or over a period of hundreds of years.

Vocabulary in Context. How accurate are you in using words you think you already know? Do you know that the word *exotic* means "a thing or person from a foreign country?" So, exotic flowers and exotic dancers are flowers and dancers from a foreign country. Exotic has been used incorrectly so often and for so long that it has developed a second meaning. Most people use exotic to mean "strikingly unusual, as in color or design."

Many people think that the words *imply* and *infer* mean the same thing. They do not. An author may imply, or suggest, something. The reader then infers what the author implied. In other words, to imply is to suggest an idea. To infer is to take meaning out.

It would be easy to see what would happen to a passage if a reader skipped a word or two that he or she did not know, and imposed fuzzy meanings on a few others. The result would inevitably be a gross misunderstanding of the author's message. You will become a better reader if you learn the exact meanings and different shades of meaning of the words that are already familiar to you.

Answering the Main Idea Question

The main idea questions in this book are not the usual multiple-choice variety from which you must select the one correct statement. Rather, you are given three statements and are asked to select the statement that expresses the main idea of the passage, the statement that is too narrow, and the statement that is too broad. You have to work hard and actively to identify all three statements correctly. This new type of question teaches you the differences among statements that, at first, seem almost equal.

To help you handle these questions, let's go behind the scenes to see how the main idea questions in this book were constructed. The true main idea statement was always written first. It had to be neat, succinct, and positive. The main idea tells who or what the subject of the passage is. It also answers the question does what? or is what? Next, keeping the main idea statement in mind, the other two statements were written. They are variations of the main idea statement. The too narrow statement had to be in line with the main idea, but express only part of it. Likewise, the too broad statement had to be in line with the main idea, but to be too general in scope.

Read the sample passage that starts below. Then, to learn how to answer the main idea questions, follow the instructions in the box. The answer to each part of the question has been filled in for you. The score for each answer has also been marked.

Sample Passage

Silk is fancy cloth that is much softer than cotton. Silk is made by the silkworm caterpillar. When full grown, the caterpillar weaves a cocoon of silk strands. It makes a sticky gum to hold the threads together. Long ago, in ancient China, people discovered how to wash the gum away. This made it possible for them to unwind the silk threads and weave them into cloth. The shimmering fabric could be dyed many colors. The process of making silk fabric was a Chinese secret for 2000 years. The Chinese sold silk to the rest of the world. But silkworms were eventually smuggled out of China. Now silk is made in many places around the world. The tiny silkworm is now part of a big industry.

Main Idea	1		Answer	Score
	Mark the *main idea*		M	15
	Mark the statement that is *too broad*		B	5
	Mark the statement that is *too narrow*		N	5

a. Silkworms make silk thread that can be woven into beautiful cloth.　　　　　M　　15

[This statement is the main idea. It gathers all the important points of the passage. It tells (1) that the passage is about the silkworm, (2) that the silkworm makes silk thread, and (3) that the thread is woven into beautiful cloth.]

b. Silkworms make silk.　　　　　B　　5

[This statement is too broad. Although the sentence is true, it leaves out some important points. We don't know (1) what form the silk takes when it is made, or (2) what the silk is used for.]

c. Silkworms spin silk cocoons.　　　　　N　　5

[This sentence is too narrow. It tells us only part of the story. It completely ignores the fact that the silkworm's silk is made into cloth.]

Getting the Most Out of This Book

The following steps could be called "tricks of the trade." Your teachers might call them "rules for learning." It doesn't matter what they are called. What does matter is that they work.

Think About the Title. A famous language expert told me a "trick" to use when I read. "The first thing to do is to read the title. Then spend a few moments thinking about it."

Writers spend much time thinking up good titles. They try to pack a lot of meaning into them. It makes sense, then, for you to spend a few seconds trying to dig out some meaning. These few moments of thought will give you a head start on a passage.

Thinking about the title can help you in another way, too. It helps you concentrate on a passage before you begin reading. Why does this happen? Thinking about the title fills your head full of thoughts about the passage. There's no room for anything else to get in to break concentration.

The Dot System. Here is a method that will speed up your reading. It also builds comprehension at the same time.

Spend a few moments with the title. Then read quickly through the passage. Next, without looking back, answer the six questions by placing a dot in the box next to each answer of your choice. The dots will be your "unofficial" answers. For the main idea question (question one) place your dot in the box next to the statement that you think is the main idea.

The dot system helps by making you think hard on your first, fast reading. The practice you gain by trying to grasp and remember ideas makes you a stronger reader.

The Check-Mark System. First, answer the main idea question. Follow the steps that are given above each set of statements for this question. Use a capital letter to mark your final answer to each part of the main idea question.

You have answered the other five questions with a dot. Now read the passage once more carefully. This time, mark your final answer to each question by placing a check mark (✓) in the box next to the answer of your choice. The answers with the check marks are the ones that will count toward your score.

The Diagnostic Chart. Now move your final answers to the Diagnostic Chart that starts on page 207.

Use the row of boxes beside Passage 1 for the answers to the first passage. Use the row of boxes beside Passage 2 for the answers to the second passage, and so on. Write the letter of your answer to the left of the dotted line in each block.

Correct your answers using the Answer Key on pages 203–206. When scoring your answers, do not use an *x* for incorrect or a *c* for correct. Instead, use this method. If your choice is incorrect, write the letter of the correct answer to the right of the dotted line in the block.

Thus, the row of answers for each passage will show your incorrect answers. And it will also show the correct answers.

Your Total Comprehension Score. Go back to the passage you have just read. If you answered a question incorrectly, draw a line under the correct choice on the question page. Then write your score for each question on the line provided. Add the scores to get your total comprehension score. Enter that number in the box marked Total Score.

Graphing Your Progress. After you have found your total comprehension score, turn to the Progress Graph that begins on page 211. Write your score in the box under the number of the passage. Then put an *x* along the line above the box to show your total comprehension score. Join the *x*'s as you go. This will plot a line showing your progress.

Taking Corrective Action. Your incorrect answers give you a way to teach yourself how to read better. Take the time to study your wrong answers.

Go back to the questions. For each question you got wrong, read the correct answer (the one you have underlined) several times. With the correct answer in mind, go back to the passage itself. Read to see why the approved answer is better. Try to see where you made your mistake. Try to figure out why you chose a wrong answer.

The Steps in a Nutshell

Here's a quick review of the steps to follow. Following these steps is the way to get the most out of this book. Be sure you have read and understood everything in the "To the Student" section on pages ix–xvii before you start.

1. **Think About the Title of the Passage.** Try to get all the meaning the writer put into it.
2. **Read the Passage Quickly.**
3. **Answer the Questions, Using the Dot System.** Use dots to mark your unofficial answers. Don't look back at the passage.
4. **Read the Passage Again—Carefully.**
5. **Mark Your Final Answers.** Put a check mark (✓) in the box to note your final answer. Use capital letters for each part of the main idea question.

6. **Mark Your Answers on the Diagnostic Chart.** Record your final answers on the Diagnostic Chart that begins on page 207. Write your answers to the left of the dotted line in the answer blocks for the passage.

7. **Correct Your Answers.** Use the Answer Key on pages 203–206. If an answer is not correct, write the correct answer in the right side of the block, beside your wrong answer. Then go back to the question page. Place a line under the correct answer.

8. **Find Your Total Comprehension Score.** Find this by adding up the points you earned for each question. Enter the total in the box marked Total Score.

9. **Graph Your Progress.** Enter and plot your score on the graph that begins on page 211.

10. **Take Corrective Action.** Read your wrong answers. Read the passage once more. Try to figure out why you were wrong.

To the Instructor

The Reading Passages

Each of the 100 passages included in the book had to meet the following three criteria: high interest level, appropriate readability level, and factual content.

The high interest level was assured by choosing passages of mature content that would appeal to a wide range of readers.

The passages in *Six-Way Paragraphs, Introductory Level* range from reading level 1 through reading level 4, with 25 passages at each level. *Six-Way Paragraphs, Middle Level* contains passages that range from reading level 4 to reading level 8, with 20 passages at each reading level. The passages in *Six-Way Paragraphs, Advanced Level* range from reading level 8 to reading level 12, with 20 passages at each reading level.

The factual content was a definite requirement because by reading factual passages students build not only their reading skills but, of equal importance, their informational backgrounds.

The Six Questions

This book is organized around six essential questions. The most important of these is the main idea question, which is actually a set of three statements. Students must first choose and label the statement that expresses the main idea of the passage; then they must label each of the other statements as being either too narrow or too broad to be the main idea.

In addition to the main idea question, there are five other questions. These questions are within the framework of the following five categories: subject matter, supporting details, conclusions, clarifying devices, and vocabulary in context.

By repeated practice with the questions within these six categories, students will develop an active, searching attitude that will carry over to the reading of other expository prose. These six types of questions will help them become aware of what they are reading at the time they are actually seeing the words and phrases on a page. This type of thinking-while-reading sets the stage for higher comprehension and better retention.

The Diagnostic Chart

The Diagnostic Chart provides the most dignified form of guidance yet devised. With this chart, no one has to point out a student's weaknesses. The chart does that automatically, yielding the information directly and personally to the student, making self-teaching possible. The organization of the questions and the format for marking answers on the chart are what make it work so well.

The six questions for each passage are always in the same order. For example, the question designed to teach the skill of drawing conclusions is always the fourth question, and the main idea question is always first. Keeping the questions in a set order sets the stage for the smooth working of the chart.

The chart works automatically when students write the letter of their answer choices for each passage in the spaces provided. Even after completing only one passage, the chart will reveal the type or types of questions answered correctly, as well as the types answered incorrectly. As the answers for more passages are recorded, the chart will show the types of questions that are missed consistently. A pattern can be seen after three or more passages have been completed. For example, if a student answers question 4 (drawing conclusions) incorrectly for three out of four passages, the student's weakness in this area shows up automatically.

Once a weakness is revealed, have your students take the following steps: First, turn to the instructional pages in the beginning of the book, and study the section in which the topic is discussed. Second, go back and reread the questions that were missed in that particular category. Then, with the correct answer to a question in mind, read the entire passage again, trying to see how the author developed the answer to the question. Do this for each question that was missed. Third, when reading future passages, make an extra effort to correctly answer the questions in that particular category. Fourth, if the difficulty continues, arrange to see the instructor.

1 The King of Beasts

Who is the "King of Beasts"? We all know the answer. It is the lion. A male lion weighs from 350 to 400 pounds. A few weigh up to 500 pounds. Most males are about nine feet long. That's from tip of nose to tip of tail. Most are about three-and-a-half feet tall. That is at the shoulders. Females are smaller. They weigh 250 to 300 pounds. They are about eight feet long. Lions live 20 to 25 years in a zoo. How long in the jungle? No one knows.

Lions are powerful. The power is in the shoulders and forelegs. Each paw has long, sharp claws. These claws hook into prey. The lion's weight drags down the prey. Then the four long canine teeth go to work. The teeth <u>fasten</u> onto the throat. The lion has no chewing type teeth. So it uses its canine teeth. They rip the flesh into chunks. Then the chunks are swallowed whole.

Lions live in groups. The groups are called prides. A pride will have one to three adult males, several females, and cubs. Life within a pride is peaceful. Lions usually spend about 20 hours a day sleeping or resting. After a big meal, they may rest for 24 hours.

Lions prefer large prey. They hunt zebra, antelope, and buffalo. All these animals can run faster than the lion. So how does the lion catch them? Answer: by surprise. The lion creeps as close as possible first. Then it jumps. Lions often hunt at night. At night their eyes can see in the dark. Also, they can creep up closer to surprise their prey. A killed animal is dragged to a shady spot. (One lion can drag a 600 pound zebra. It would take six men to do the same.) Then the whole pride eats together. A male can eat about 75 pounds of meat in one meal. What a meal!

Main Idea	1		Answer	Score
	Mark the *main idea*		M	15
	Mark the statement that is *too broad*		B	5
	Mark the statement that is *too narrow*		N	5

a. The lion is known as the King of Beasts. ☐ _____

b. Lions have long, powerful claws. ☐ _____

c. Lions are powerful animals that are good hunters. ☐ _____

Score 15 points for each correct answer.   Score

Subject Matter   **2**   This passage is mostly about
                     ☐ a. animals in the cat family.
                     ☐ b. how lions' bodies are designed for eating and
                          hunting.
                     ☐ c. the way lions eat their food without chewing.
                     ☐ d. the differences between male and female lions.   _____

Supporting   **3**   The lion hunts its prey by
Details   ☐ a. using its speed.
                     ☐ b. creeping up on them.
                     ☐ c. only hunting at night.
                     ☐ d. hunting with the pride.   _____

Conclusion   **4**   We can conclude from this passage that
                     ☐ a. the lion is the "king" because of its size.
                     ☐ b. lions never sleep during the day.
                     ☐ c. one zebra could feed a pride.
                     ☐ d. female lions work harder than male lions.   _____

Clarifying   **5**   The writer tells how the lion's teeth "rip flesh
Devices   into chunks" in order to
                     ☐ a. explain how powerful its teeth are.
                     ☐ b. scare the reader.
                     ☐ c. contrast the lion with the cat.
                     ☐ d. show why lions hunt at night.   _____

Vocabulary   **6**   In this passage <u>fasten</u> means
in Context   ☐ a. pull.
                     ☐ b. snap.
                     ☐ c. attach.
                     ☐ d. lock.   _____

Add your scores for questions 1–6. Enter the total here   **Total**
and on the graph on page 211.   **Score**   _____

3

2 The Staff of Life

When hungry, what do you think of? Some want a thick steak. Others want a crusty loaf of French bread. I don't know about you. But I'd vote for bread. It is food that people never tire of.

Bread is a baked product made of dough. In our day, yeast is what makes it rise. The yeast ferments. It forms gas bubbles. These bubbles are trapped in the dough. These bubbles raise the bread. They give it lightness.

We know about early breads. Records show they were flat, heavy slabs. The breads were made of wild seeds, nuts, or acorns. Native Americans on the Pacific slopes still pound acorns into a form of flour. Then they make bread. Even yeast would not make such a heavy bread light.

Besides yeast, what makes bread rise? First, a flour with protein in it. Wheat or rye are often used. Start by grinding the seeds. This makes a coarse flour. Next, add water. How much water? About 60 to 65 percent of the flour's weight. Water added to flour forms gluten. Gluten must be there for the dough to rise. It forms a network throughout the dough. The dough is now elastic. It can expand. It can now hold the bubbles formed by yeast. These bubbles are carbon dioxide.

Good, smooth, light bread is rather recent. Two <u>techniques</u> made it possible. First, it used to be that wheat was ground between 2 stones. The stones would wear away. So the flour would have grit in it. A Swiss inventor crushed wheat between steel rollers. This got rid of grit. Second, Charles Fleischmann made yeast easy to use. He formed it into cakes. This was in 1915.

Fresh bread and butter. You can't beat it.

Main Idea	1		
		Answer	Score
	Mark the *main idea*	M	15
	Mark the statement that is *too broad*	B	5
	Mark the statement that is *too narrow*	N	5
	a. Early breads were made from wild seeds or nuts.	☐	_____
	b. For many years people have made, baked, and eaten bread.	☐	_____
	c. Bread has been around for a long time, but the process for making it has changed.	☐	_____

Score 15 points for each correct answer.   **Score**

Subject Matter **2** What is the main subject of this passage?
- ☐ a. baking bread
- ☐ b. bread ingredients
- ☐ c. making bread
- ☐ d. rising dough   _____

Supporting
Details **3** To make bread one needs
- ☐ a. yeast.
- ☐ b. flour.
- ☐ c. wheat.
- ☐ d. seeds.   _____

Conclusion **4** You can figure out from this passage
- ☐ a. bread has been enjoyed for many years.
- ☐ b. the techniques for making bread have not changed.
- ☐ c. bread cannot be enjoyed without butter.
- ☐ d. without bread we could not live.   _____

Clarifying
Devices **5** The author uses a process to explain how
- ☐ a. Indians made flour.
- ☐ b. to grind wheat.
- ☐ c. to make smooth loaves.
- ☐ d. bread rises.   _____

Vocabulary
in Context **6** In this passage the word <u>techniques</u> means
- ☐ a. plans.
- ☐ b. methods.
- ☐ c. problems.
- ☐ d. answers.   _____

Add your scores for questions 1–6. Enter the total here   **Total**
and on the graph on page 211.   **Score**   _____

3 Getting a Good Night's Sleep

Good sleep is needed for good health. During sleep, your body repairs itself. Your immune system is built up. Don't shortchange yourself of the sleep you need. Here are some of an expert's tips for getting a good night's sleep.

1. Make sure your room is dark. Pull down the shades. Let no light of any kind in.

2. Before you go to sleep, ask your family not to turn on a light. Light breaks the sleep rhythm. Once broken, it's hard to get the sleep clock running right. As a result, you will not sleep well. You will wake up tired.

3. A hot bath just before bed is good. It makes you relax. You are at peace. This starts the desire for sleep.

4. During the day, get some exercise. Even a mild <u>program</u> will show good results. How about a good long walk? This will get your body to work. You will find that toward evening you will get that nice, tired feeling. Sleep then will come easily. Added to this, exercise is good for your health.

5. Here is what to do when you get up. Open the shades or blinds. Let the sun in. Open the windows. Let the fresh air in. This sun and air get imprinted on your brain. The rhythm of being awake gets started. Your body clock is set for the day. That clock will let you know when it is the right time to go to sleep.

Main Idea	1		
		Answer	**Score**
	Mark the _main idea_	M	15
	Mark the statement that is _too broad_	B	5
	Mark the statement that is _too narrow_	N	5

a. Good sleep is all that is needed to be healthy. ☐ _____

b. Light breaks the sleep pattern and stops sound sleep. ☐ _____

c. To get good sleep and stay healthy follow five important steps. ☐ _____

Score 15 points for each correct answer. Score

Subject Matter **2** This passage focuses on
☐ a. a study of sleep patterns.
☐ b. good health.
☐ c. rules and steps.
☐ d. how to get good sleep.

_____

Supporting Details **3** To get good sleep you need
☐ a. warm sheets.
☐ b. a soft bed.
☐ c. a dark room.
☐ d. fresh air.

_____

Conclusion **4** The passage suggests that it is important to
☐ a. not go to bed too early.
☐ b. get sleepy before you go to bed.
☐ c. get up early in the morning.
☐ d. exercise before you go to sleep.

_____

Clarifying Devices **5** In the first paragraph, the phrase "shortchange yourself" means that you
☐ a. need not have a lot of change or money to sleep well.
☐ b. cannot follow the steps.
☐ c. cheat yourself.
☐ d. should look at yourself.

_____

Vocabulary in Context **6** In this passage program means
☐ a. a television show.
☐ b. plan.
☐ c. list of speakers at a meeting.
☐ d. something that runs on a computer.

_____

Add your scores for questions 1–6. Enter the total here and on the graph on page 211. Total Score _____

4 The Longest Trail

Listen carefully. Don't answer too quickly. At least, don't say "yes" too soon. A friend might ask, "Want to take a hike?" You should say, "Where?" If he replies, "The entire Appalachian Trail," take warning. Here's why.

The trail is the longest marked footpath in the world. It starts at Springer Mountain, Georgia. It winds along the crest of the mountains. It goes through 14 states. It ends at Mt. Katahdin, Maine. As the crow flies, this is about 2,200 miles. But when walked, the trail is 2,600 miles. If done nonstop, it takes about six months.

Most hikers begin from Springer Mountain. They start around April 1. This is why. The snow has probably melted in the south. But there may still be snow in the north. By the time they reach Maine, the snow will be long gone. What's the chance of making it nonstop? Here are the <u>data</u>. About 1,500 attempt it each year. About 300 make it. It is a great challenge.

Careful planning is necessary. There are problems to solve. The biggest is weight on one's back. Too many hikers start out with too much. Wise ones don't carry food. They send packages to post offices along the way. There are no camp fires allowed. Some shelters are near the path. But the trail is crowded. It is hard to find space. A perfect tent is necessary. And it rains a lot. Great rain gear is needed. It should be light.

Benton MacKaye founded the trail. The first part was cut in 1922. It is cared for by volunteers in each state. Do you plan to go? Read lots of books by people who've done it.

Main Idea	1		
		Answer	Score
	Mark the *main idea*	M	15
	Mark the statement that is *too broad*	B	5
	Mark the statement that is *too narrow*	N	5

a. Hiking the entire Appalachian Trail takes about six months. ☐ ____

b. There are many long trails for hiking. ☐ ____

c. It is a challenge to hike the Appalachian Trail. ☐ ____

Score 15 points for each correct answer.   **Score**

Subject Matter   **2** The focus of this passage is
    ☐ a. hiking trails.
    ☐ b. the longest trails in the world.
    ☐ c. dangers of hiking in the Appalachian
        Mountains.
    ☐ d. hiking the Appalachian Trail.   _____

Supporting   **3** To hike the Appalachian Trail one must
Details   ☐ a. bring many books.
    ☐ b. plan ahead.
    ☐ c. wear heavy clothing.
    ☐ d. have a strong mule.   _____

Conclusion   **4** The author of this passage
    ☐ a. has hiked the entire trail many times.
    ☐ b. has volunteered to maintain the trail.
    ☐ c. admires those who enjoy hiking.
    ☐ d. thinks hiking the trail is difficult but
        rewarding.   _____

Clarifying   **5** The phrase "As the crow flies" is used to refer to
Devices   the trail's
    ☐ a. distance.
    ☐ b. height.
    ☐ c. view.
    ☐ d. difficulty.   _____

Vocabulary   **6** The word <u>data</u> means
in Context   ☐ a. untrue stories.
    ☐ b. volunteers.
    ☐ c. pieces of information.
    ☐ d. distances.   _____

Add your scores for questions 1–6. Enter the total here   **Total**
and on the graph on page 211.   **Score**   _____

5 The Arabian Horse

Arabs have always loved horses. They spent years breeding the best. And they won blue ribbons. But they did not rely on ribbons. Stronger proof showed they were best. The proof was this. Their horses were chosen by the world's breeders. The breeders would buy a horse. This horse was the stud. They would use it to breed others. In this way, breeders got a head start. They started with a great horse. They reaped the work of years of Arab breeding.

What makes this horse so good? Here are some of the good points. The bones of the horse are as dense as ivory. So it has fewer leg problems. The U.S. Army put horses to a 300-mile test. Only 15 percent of the pure Arabians had leg problems. Of pure thoroughbred horses, 90 percent came down with sore legs.

How about a test for endurance? The Arabian horse went miles. It carried a heavy load too. It just did not tire. Why? It took an X-ray to give the answer. The horse has a short back. It has one bone less than other horses. This gives it a strong back. This gives it a straight back. That's why it can carry a heavy load.

It is hard to find a horse with so many good points. There is still a further good point. The horse is a beauty. The beauty comes from the way the horse is put together. The proportions are perfect. There is no part in excess. There are no extremes. All parts are in perfect balance. The neck is set just right. The flaring nostrils take in air easily. The rib cage holds lots of air. This makes long distances easy to travel. The Arab breeders did a perfect job.

Main Idea	1			Answer	Score
		Mark the *main idea*		M	15
		Mark the statement that is *too broad*		B	5
		Mark the statement that is *too narrow*		N	5

a. Careful breeding can make horses perfect. ☐ _____

b. Arabian horses have fewer backbones than other horses. ☐ _____

c. The Arabian horse was bred to be strong and tireless. ☐ _____

Score 15 points for each correct answer.

Subject Matter **2** This passage centers on the Arabian horse's
- [ ] a. strong bone structure.
- [ ] b. physical build.
- [ ] c. healthy nature.
- [ ] d. character traits. _____

Supporting Details **3** The Arabian horse is admired for its
- [ ] a. gentleness.
- [ ] b. intelligence.
- [ ] c. rarity.
- [ ] d. perfection. _____

Conclusion **4** Details in the passage suggest that the Arabian horse is not
- [ ] a. large.
- [ ] b. beautiful.
- [ ] c. strong.
- [ ] d. useful. _____

Clarifying Devices **5** By saying that the Arabian's bones are "as dense as ivory," the author implies that the bones are
- [ ] a. thick and strong.
- [ ] b. soft and flexible.
- [ ] c. light and brittle.
- [ ] d. pure and fine. _____

Vocabulary in Context **6** As used in this passage, <u>reaped</u> means
- [ ] a. stole.
- [ ] b. found.
- [ ] c. gained.
- [ ] d. borrowed. _____

Add your scores for questions 1–6. Enter the total here and on the graph on page 211.

Total Score _____

6 All About Tea

Which country grows the most tea? The answer is India. It grows three times as much as China. Which country drinks the most tea? It's neither China nor Japan. It's Great Britain.

In the wild, tea plants may be 30 feet tall. But a plant grown for market is pruned. Pruning keeps the plant only three or four feet tall. This is an easy height for tea plucking. Only the two top leaves and bud of each new shoot are plucked. So to make money, tea plantations must be huge.

In general, there are two kinds of tea. Black tea and green tea. Black tea is fermented. In the process, the tea loses nearly all of its healthy qualities. Green tea is steamed right after the leaves are picked. Green tea retains its healthy qualities. For instance, it may prevent heart disease.

How did we get tea bags? The answer: by accident. Tea merchants used to send samples in tin boxes. This was costly. One merchant thought of a cheaper way. He sent samples in small silk bags. Customers would snip open the bag. They would brew the leaves as usual. One customer put the bag into a pot. Then he just poured hot water over it. And the tea bag was born.

Shen Nung was the first to drink tea. (Shen was a Chinese emperor.) This was about 2737 B.C. Shen had bad digestion. So he drank several cups of hot water daily. One day something happened. Leaves from a wild tea tree fell into the hot water pot. The next cup was poured. The water was now colored. Shen sipped it. He liked it. He drank it all. Shen was proud of his new drink. He served it to his guests. Word spread. People thought this way. Tea is good enough for the Emperor. So it must be good enough for the people. Tea became the drink of China.

Main Idea 1		
	Answer	Score
Mark the *main idea*	M	15
Mark the statement that is *too broad*	B	5
Mark the statement that is *too narrow*	N	5

a. Green tea and black tea are not made the same way.	☐	____
b. Tea is enjoyed by people all over the world.	☐	____
c. Tea was discovered centuries ago, but it is still grown and is drunk today.	☐	____

Subject Matter **2** Another good title for this passage might be
- ☐ a. An Ancient Drink.
- ☐ b. Green Tea.
- ☐ c. A Favorite Drink for Centuries.
- ☐ d. Tea Plant.   _____

Supporting Details **3** One difference between green and black tea is that green tea
- ☐ a. comes from a different plant.
- ☐ b. has a better taste.
- ☐ c. is grown on more tea plantations.
- ☐ d. is healthier.   _____

Conclusion **4** One can conclude from this passage that tea
- ☐ a. from India is the best.
- ☐ b. is better for you than any other drink.
- ☐ c. is popular in many countries.
- ☐ d. only grows in warm climates.   _____

Clarifying Devices **5** The author's main purpose in writing this passage is to
- ☐ a. convince you.
- ☐ b. make you laugh.
- ☐ c. tell you how to do something.
- ☐ d. give you information.   _____

Vocabulary in Context **6** In this passage <u>retains</u> means
- ☐ a. keeps.
- ☐ b. makes.
- ☐ c. brings forth.
- ☐ d. loses.   _____

Add your scores for questions 1–6. Enter the total here and on the graph on page 211.   **Total Score**   _____

7 The Pacific Salmon

Salmon are born in fresh water. But they spend their entire adult life in the salty sea. At sea, a salmon feeds on small creatures. These are a kind of tiny shrimp. The shrimp are called "pink feed." This feed probably gives color to the pink meat of a salmon.

The sea is filled with food. But it is filled with enemies too. Some of these are seals, sharks, and sea bass. Salmon make a tasty meal, so they're not safe anywhere. Down deep, the lamprey eels dwell. They gobble up many salmon. There's no safety at the surface either. Sea birds swoop down. They carry many salmon away.

All salmon are not alike. There are four main ones. One is the chinook. A big one weighs 100 or more pounds. A fish like this would snap your rod. Second, there's the sockeye. It weighs about five pounds. Its flesh is deep red. This is the most important commercial salmon. It yields the highest dollar value. Pink salmon are the smallest. They weigh about three to seven pounds. Most pinks are canned. They have a delicate flavor. Fourth is the coho. Its flesh is medium red. It weighs about nine pounds. Some that stay out at sea longer weigh more. They can be 25 pounds.

Salmon travel far. They may go thousands of miles. Most travel for three years. They were born in the headwaters of some stream. They were five inches long then. That's when they first poked their noses into the sea. But they have swum far away from their place of birth.

Now, here's the big mystery. The salmon turn back. Why do they do this? Some call it the "homing instinct." The salmon move back toward the fresh water in which their life began.

Main Idea 1

	Answer	Score
Mark the *main idea*	M	15
Mark the statement that is *too broad*	B	5
Mark the statement that is *too narrow*	N	5

a. Pacific salmon travel in the sea for about three years. ☐ _____

b. There are different types of salmon, but all spend a few years living in the sea. ☐ _____

c. All salmon follow a very specific life journey. ☐ _____

Score 15 points for each correct answer. **Score**

Subject Matter   **2**   This passage is about
- [ ] a. fish of the Pacific.
- [ ] b. the salmon and its life.
- [ ] c. the Chinook and coho salmon.
- [ ] d. freshwater fish.

_____

Supporting Details   **3**   The sockeye and the pink salmon are different because of their
- [ ] a. skin color.
- [ ] b. length.
- [ ] c. stay at sea.
- [ ] d. strength.

_____

Conclusion   **4**   We can assume that salmon
- [ ] a. attack other fish.
- [ ] b. taste like shrimp.
- [ ] c. like fresh water better than salt water.
- [ ] d. are strong swimmers.

_____

Clarifying Devices   **5**   The term "homing instinct" means
- [ ] a. a natural need to return home.
- [ ] b. wanting to stay home.
- [ ] c. a way of recognizing surroundings.
- [ ] d. trying to go back home.

_____

Vocabulary in Context   **6**   The word <u>yields</u>, as used in the passage, means
- [ ] a. brings in.
- [ ] b. catches.
- [ ] c. stops.
- [ ] d. spends.

_____

Add your scores for questions 1–6. Enter the total here and on the graph on page 211.

Total Score _____

8 The Long Way Home

The "homing instinct" drives the salmon great distances. The fish may be a thousand miles from home. It is probably off the coast of Chile or Peru. Suddenly, it heads northward. It is looking for the freshwater stream where it was spawned. Hundreds of streams flow into the sea. All of them contain fresh water. All are very much like the stream where the salmon was born. But it passes all these. It swims day and night, mile after mile. But then it takes a right turn. There is no hesitation. "This is my home stream," it seems to think. "I can smell it." This is the mystery. The fish was five inches long when it left. It weighed about a pound. It was gone about three years. How does it know exactly where to go? Now a new vigor enters its body. Rapids and waterfalls cannot stop it. It leaps and swims against the current. It can leap ten feet. It can leap into a waterfall and with its powerful tail leap again. If it fails the first time, it tries over and over.

There are men on the banks with rods. The salmon ignores all bait and food. It has only one mission in mind. It swims to find the clear water of its birth. It will find it. Not by sight. But by taste and smell.

The salmon is now upstream. Here the water does not run so swiftly. The salmon is almost home. "Here is my side streamlet," it seems to think. The water is just a few feet deep. Finally the trip is over. But the salmon does not rest. Instead, it starts its nest. The nest is called a *redd*. The salmon's tail and body swish hard. Mud, plants, and stones are scattered by the movement. The salmon clears a spot five to six feet across. Now a "clean and dustless" nest can be built.

Main Idea 1

	Answer	Score
Mark the *main idea*	M	15
Mark the statement that is *too broad*	B	5
Mark the statement that is *too narrow*	N	5

a. The salmon is able to leap high into the air to get upstream. ☐ _____

b. It is a mystery how salmon get back home. ☐ _____

c. Salmon are able to find their way back to their original home to make a nest. ☐ _____

Score 15 points for each correct answer.   **Score**

Subject Matter   **2**   Another good title for this passage would be
- [ ] a. How the Salmon Builds a Nest.
- [ ] b. The Salmon's Homing Instinct.
- [ ] c. A Great Fish.
- [ ] d. Swimming Upstream.   _____

Supporting   **3**   In the salmon's trip to get home it
Details
- [ ] a. loses weight.
- [ ] b. stops to smell fishermen's bait.
- [ ] c. swims against the water's current.
- [ ] d. can leap 20 feet in the air.   _____

Conclusion   **4**   For the salmon, the trip home is
- [ ] a. exciting.
- [ ] b. difficult.
- [ ] c. lonely.
- [ ] d. frightening.   _____

Clarifying   **5**   To make this passage interesting the author
Devices
- [ ] a. uses only facts.
- [ ] b. tells a humorous story.
- [ ] c. includes the fish's thoughts and feelings.
- [ ] d. includes famous quotes.   _____

Vocabulary   **6**   In this passage, <u>spawned</u> means
in Context
- [ ] a. spotted.
- [ ] b. nesting.
- [ ] c. caught.
- [ ] d. born.   _____

Add your scores for questions 1–6. Enter the total here   **Total**
and on the graph on page 211.   **Score**   _____

9 Completing the Life Cycle

On the trip home, the male salmon stays with his mate. They travel north together for thousands of miles. They jump the same rapids. They hurdle the same waterfalls. When she builds a new nest, he protects it. Other females are looking for a nesting spot. But the male keeps them away.

The female doesn't rest. She <u>hovers</u> over the nest. She contracts. The eggs come out. Dozens at a time form a stream. The nest is quickly covered by about 10,000 eggs. Also quickly, the male darts over the eggs. He gives off a milky mist called *milt*. This milt fertilizes the eggs.

Then a strange thing happens. The parents don't stay around. They're exhausted. They relax. They let themselves float downstream. Soon they die and are washed ashore. But this is not a waste. Hungry bears already line the shore. They eat and get fatter and fatter. Soon they will be ready for their winter's sleep.

What about the eggs? They will lay in the nest for about $2^1/_2$ months. About that time, there will be a wiggle in the eggs. Then the young, called *fry*, burst forth. Each fry now has a yolk sac under its chin. This sac provides food. Now the fry hide among the reeds and weeds. They feed off the sac for a few weeks. Then, after about ten weeks, they look like fish. They stay in the fresh water a few months longer. Then the strong urge comes. The salmon are vigorous and lively. They are five inches long now. They are ready to leave the friendly fresh water. Its taste and smell will stay in their brains. The memories will be there for the salmon's whole life cycle. They will be there until the salmon becomes food for the bears lined up on the shore.

Main Idea	1			Answer	Score
		Mark the *main idea*		M	15
		Mark the statement that is *too broad*		B	5
		Mark the statement that is *too narrow*		N	5

a. Salmon lay eggs that will follow the same life cycle as their parents did. ☐ _____

b. The male and female salmon leave their eggs and go downstream to die. ☐ _____

c. Salmon life follows a pattern. ☐ _____

Score 15 points for each correct answer.   **Score**

Subject Matter   **2**   This passage is mainly about

☐ a. the behavior of male and female salmon.

☐ b. fertilizing salmon eggs.

☐ c. the beginning and end of a salmon's life.

☐ d. the death of the salmon.   _____

Supporting   **3**   The "fry" stays alive because
Details

☐ a. its parents provide it with food.

☐ b. it feeds off weeds.

☐ c. its yolk sac provides it with food.

☐ d. it stays in the fresh water for a few months.   _____

Conclusion   **4**   From this passage you can conclude that

☐ a. laying and fertilizing eggs takes a lot of effort.

☐ b. most salmon are eaten by bears.

☐ c. fish worry about what will happen to their young.

☐ d. salmon stay in fresh water for a year.   _____

Clarifying   **5**   In the final paragraph, "the strong urge" is to
Devices

☐ a. mate.

☐ b. leave the fresh water.

☐ c. lay eggs.

☐ d. stay away from the bears.   _____

Vocabulary   **6**   In this passage <u>hovers</u> means
in Context

☐ a. stays in one place.

☐ b. cries.

☐ c. returns.

☐ d. stands off to the side.   _____

Add your scores for questions 1–6. Enter the total here   **Total**

and on the graph on page 211.   **Score**   _____

10 The Lone Eagle

Could you stay awake for 33½ hours? That's a long time. Not even a few seconds to doze are allowed. The "Lone Eagle" did it. Who is he? He is Charles A. Lindbergh.

It was spring 1927. The grassy field was soaked with rain. The tires were sinking into the turf. The plane was loaded with tons of gasoline. It was just enough to get to Paris.

The Lone Eagle gunned the engine to get maximum power. He knew the plane was heavy with gas. The soggy turf would make it hard to gain take-off speed.

The Lone Eagle waved a signal. The wheel blocks were jerked away. The plane lurched forward. The soggy turf did not let go easily. Would he gain enough speed? Would there be enough runway? The trees at the end were already close—too close.

It was too late to stop. He pulled the stick back hard. Luckily the plane lifted. The wheels skimmed the top leaves. Prayerful cheers of relief rose from the ground crew. The Lone Eagle quickly waved. He turned northward. First he crossed Long Island Sound. Then he headed to Labrador. The plane was to fly over land as long as possible. Just in case.

Then it was all water. He was over the North Atlantic. Ice formed on his wings. The Lone Eagle skimmed the waves. It was warmer there. The ice melted.

Thirty-three hours passed. He saw the lights of Paris. He circled. Over 100,000 people crowded the airstrip. He circled again. He found a clear airstrip. He landed. A <u>battalion</u> of police moved in. They had to keep the wild crowd at bay. Everyone wanted to see the hero. He was the first to fly across the ocean alone.

Main Idea   1

	Answer	Score
Mark the *main idea*	M	15
Mark the statement that is *too broad*	B	5
Mark the statement that is *too narrow*	N	5

a. The "Lone Eagle" was Charles A. Lindbergh. ☐ _____

b. Luck and endurance made the "Lone Eagle's" trip possible. ☐ _____

c. The "Lone Eagle" made a memorable flight in 1927. ☐ _____

Subject Matter   **2**   This selection is mostly about the "Lone Eagle's"

    ☐ a. flight to Paris.

    ☐ b. desire to be alone.

    ☐ c. preparation for flying.

    ☐ d. ability to stay awake.   _____

Supporting Details   **3**   During Charles A. Lindbergh's flight to Paris

    ☐ a. he only flew over land.

    ☐ b. the plane almost ran out of gas.

    ☐ c. he flew over the Atlantic Ocean.

    ☐ d. snow covered the plane.   _____

Conclusion   **4**   We can assume from the passage that

    ☐ a. this was Lindbergh's first time in an airplane.

    ☐ b. flying over large bodies of water was a challenge.

    ☐ c. planes only flew over land until now.

    ☐ d. the author witnessed this event.   _____

Clarifying Devices   **5**   The writer develops suspense in the fourth paragraph by

    ☐ a. describing the plane.

    ☐ b. asking questions.

    ☐ c. using facts.

    ☐ d. recalling people's descriptions.   _____

Vocabulary in Context   **6**   In this passage <u>battalion</u> means a

    ☐ a. small gathering.

    ☐ b. large group.

    ☐ c. parade.

    ☐ d. department.   _____

Add your scores for questions 1–6. Enter the total here and on the graph on page 211.   **Total Score**   _____

11 Discovered by Accident

What was discovered by accident? The answer is penicillin. It kills germs. By killing germs, it saves lives. Suppose you are sick. You go to a doctor. She examines you. She says you have a "staph" infection. She gives you some pills. You take them. The pills knock out the staph. Soon you are well. Before penicillin, this would not happen. Staph was almost sure death.

Everyone wanted a cure. Labs worked day and night. They grew the staph in small dishes. Then they tried to kill it. Nothing worked.

The lab dishes had covers on them. These kept things from falling into a dish. Molds were a big worry. They are always floating in the air. You can't see them. They're too small. There are thousands of different molds. Molds can ruin an experiment. That's why dishes are covered.

Dr. Alexander Fleming was working to kill the staph germ. He worked for years. One day he took a cover off a dish. He looked inside. There was a thick growth of staph germ. There was also some mold. Then he saw something strange. Where the mold was, there was no growth of staph. This is what Fleming probably thought. "By accident, I found a mold to kill the <u>dreaded</u> staph."

This is how penicillin was found. But here's the real miracle. There are thousands of types of molds. But only one type can kill staph. The mold must have fallen into the dish a few days before. The cover was probably off only a few seconds. In those few seconds the right mold fell into the right dish. Another man might have thrown the dish away. What a loss this would have been. The human race was lucky. Fleming was very smart. He understood what the mold did.

Main Idea	1		Answer	Score
	Mark the *main idea*		M	15
	Mark the statement that is *too broad*		B	5
	Mark the statement that is *too narrow*		N	5

a. Dr. Fleming knew the mold growing in the staph germ dish was different. ☐ _____

b. Accidents can be helpful if the right person understands what they mean. ☐ _____

c. Without Dr. Fleming's insight the discovery of penicillin would have been lost. ☐ _____

Score 15 points for each correct answer. **Score**

Subject Matter   **2**   This passage is mainly about
    ☐ a. discovering penicillin.
    ☐ b. helpful accidents.
    ☐ c. Dr. Fleming's research.
    ☐ d. a cure for infections.   _____

Supporting
Details   **3**   To find a cure for staph infections
    ☐ a. staph was dropped into many solutions.
    ☐ b. mold was kept in small dishes.
    ☐ c. staph was grown in small dishes.
    ☐ d. covers were put over test tubes.   _____

Conclusion   **4**   The last paragraph suggests that
    ☐ a. accidents happen to everyone.
    ☐ b. luck is needed when doing scientific
        experiments.
    ☐ c. the unprepared person will miss valuable
        opportunities.
    ☐ d. the prepared person does not have accidents.   _____

Clarifying
Devices   **5**   Most of the passage is devoted to
    ☐ a. a strong argument.
    ☐ b. advice.
    ☐ c. a strange story.
    ☐ d. the results of several experiments.   _____

Vocabulary
in Context   **6**   As used in this passage, <u>dreaded</u> is closest in
meaning to
    ☐ a. well-known.
    ☐ b. feared.
    ☐ c. diseased.
    ☐ d. misunderstood.   _____

**Add your scores for questions 1–6. Enter the total here
and on the graph on page 211.**   **Total
Score**   _____

12 The Pony Express

Would you want this job? The ad was in a newspaper. "Expert riders wanted. Young, light, lean, and wiry men. Orphans are preferred." What was the job? A Pony Express rider! It may sound scary. But the pay was high for those times. It was $100 to $150 a month. Buffalo Bill went for a job. He <u>fibbed</u>. He was only 14. He got the job. His father was dead. He had a mother and family. He had to support them.

The Pony Express carried U.S. mail. The route started in Missouri. It ended in California. It covered 1,966 miles. Service began April 3, 1860. The first trip took ten days. Later trips took eight to nine days. Speed was prime. The Express had to beat the stagecoach. The coach carried mail too. But it took over 20 days.

Why was the Express so fast? The riders rode top speed. They dashed from one station to the next. Stations were 10 to 15 miles apart. A fresh horse was always ready. Riders only stopped for two minutes. Each one rode about 75 miles. They rode night and day. They went out in all kinds of weather.

The Pony Express owned 400 horses. Buyers first went through the route. They bought horses from the Native Americans. They took only the fastest. This was the secret of success.

The Express ended on October 24, 1861. It lasted only 18 months. Here is why. The telegraph was now coast to coast. News could travel even faster. But riders had gone over 650,000 miles. And the mail was lost only once. It is a great record.

Main Idea	1		
		Answer	Score
	Mark the *main idea*	M	15
	Mark the statement that is *too broad*	B	5
	Mark the statement that is *too narrow*	N	5

a. Mail was delivered by Pony Express in the middle 1800s. ☐ _____

b. Pony Express riders rode through the day and night. ☐ _____

c. The brave riders of the Pony Express delivered the mail fast and accurately. ☐ _____

Subject Matter   **2**   This passage is primarily about
       ☐ a. Buffalo Bill.
       ☐ b. the dangers of the Pony Express.
       ☐ c. delivering mail in the 1860s.
       ☐ d. the speed of the Pony Express.   _____

Supporting Details   **3**   Pony Express horses came from
       ☐ a. farms.
       ☐ b. wild country.
       ☐ c. Native Americans.
       ☐ d. stagecoaches.   _____

Conclusion   **4**   We can assume that the telegraph replaced the Pony Express because
       ☐ a. it was less dangerous.
       ☐ b. riders were not needed.
       ☐ c. it was electronic.
       ☐ d. messages could be sent faster and further.   _____

Clarifying Devices   **5**   The author uses an old advertisement in the first paragraph to give an idea of
       ☐ a. the dangers of the Pony Express.
       ☐ b. what life was like in the 1800s.
       ☐ c. the difference between past and present job advertisements.
       ☐ d. how the Pony Express found men.   _____

Vocabulary in Context   **6**   The word <u>fibbed</u> means
       ☐ a. worked.
       ☐ b. tried.
       ☐ c. failed.
       ☐ d. lied.   _____

Add your scores for questions 1–6. Enter the total here and on the graph on page 211.   **Total Score**   _____

13 The Personality of a Cat

Cats are very smart. They are one of the smartest of all tame animals. The brain of a cat is large. It is highly developed. This may be why cats have good memories. Cats remember kindness and cruelty. It is a good idea to treat a cat well. Cats can "speak" too. They meow for attention. Often they stand by a door. Then they meow. Then they look over their shoulders. They want to see if you are coming. Cats make other noises also. They purr when they are happy. They hiss when they are angry.

Cats have a lot of pride. They usually will not do silly tricks. They seem to know what is beneath them. Almost all cats want to have their own way. They are mostly true to only one person—if to anyone. They don't switch loyalty easily. Cats were free in the wild. They want to stay that way. They like to be their own masters. When a cat is left alone, it can go back to caring for itself. It can live in the wild again. This is different from dogs. Dogs will switch their loyalty. At one time dogs were loyal to the leaders of packs. Now, they will transfer <u>allegiance</u> to their owner. They do not like to be alone.

With kindness, a cat can be trained. Cats can learn to do many things. Some cats can learn to open doors. Some can ring doorbells. Some can even turn on water. Then they take a drink. Cats are very smart, though. Here is what they do before drinking. They put a paw in the water. They test whether the water is hot or cold.

Main Idea	1			
			Answer	**Score**
	Mark the *main idea*		M	15
	Mark the statement that is *too broad*		B	5
	Mark the statement that is *too narrow*		N	5
	a. Cats have some interesting qualities.		☐	_____
	b. Cats are smart but independent animals.		☐	_____
	c. Cats can be trained to do many things.		☐	_____

Subject Matter   **2**   This passage is mainly concerned with
    ☐ a. beliefs about cats.
    ☐ b. sayings about cats.
    ☐ c. the cat.
    ☐ d. differences between cats and dogs.   _____

Supporting Details   **3**   Cats are interesting to have around because
    ☐ a. they are always loyal to their owners.
    ☐ b. they like to do tricks.
    ☐ c. when they need attention they will scratch.
    ☐ d. they are smart and have good memories.   _____

Conclusion   **4**   Many cats like to be outside because they
    ☐ a. have claws and sharp teeth.
    ☐ b. like independence and freedom.
    ☐ c. can outsmart a dog.
    ☐ d. like fresh air.   _____

Clarifying Devices   **5**   The statement about cats that some tricks
are "beneath them" means that
    ☐ a. cats think they are too good to do the tricks.
    ☐ b. cats cannot easily crawl into low places.
    ☐ c. cats only like to do tricks in which they can
       stand up.
    ☐ d. cats have a very humble attitude.   _____

Vocabulary in Context   **6**   The word <u>allegiance</u> is used to mean
    ☐ a. pride.
    ☐ b. beliefs.
    ☐ c. loyalty.
    ☐ d. compassion.   _____

Add your scores for questions 1–6. Enter the total here   **Total**
and on the graph on page 211.   **Score**   _____

14 Cat Facts

Here are some interesting facts about cats. The first is about cats' vocal cords. Each cat has two sets. One cord is above the other. The lower cord produces the "meow." The upper cord produces purrs and growls. Another fact deals with cats' vision. In complete and total darkness, cats cannot see. But if there is even a <u>glimmer</u> from stars or the moon, they can see. A cat's iris can open very wide. It catches even small scraps of light.

The third fact is about cats' whiskers. Most cats have 25 to 30 whiskers. They grow in four rows from the side of the mouth. It is said that the whiskers are used for measuring. That is, a cat will not go through a hole if its whiskers touch the sides. This is not true. The whiskers are attached to nerves. They are delicate sense organs.

Cats are the cleanest of animals. You have, no doubt, watched them wash. The cat licks its paw first. Then with a wet paw it washes its face and head. Finally it cleans the rest of its body with its tongue. The tongue is special. It has a patch of sharp spines. The spines are near the tip of the tongue. These spines face backward. The tip of the tongue feels like a coarse file. So the cat grooms itself with its rasplike tongue. The tongue, like a comb, picks up loose hair. Cats often swallow these balls of hair. They can cause some stomach trouble. A vet is often needed.

All in all, a cat is smart, clean, and has lots of dignity. It will not transfer its trust to you simply because it is in your house. To get that trust, you have to earn it. The best way to do this, it seems, is with kindness.

Main Idea	1			Answer	Score
		Mark the _main idea_		**M**	15
		Mark the statement that is _too broad_		**B**	5
		Mark the statement that is _too narrow_		**N**	5

a. There are many interesting facts about cats. ☐ _____

b. A cat's tongue and paws keep it clean and groomed. ☐ _____

c. Cats have interesting physical characteristics and habits. ☐ _____

Score 15 points for each correct answer.   **Score**

Subject Matter   **2**   This selection centers on
                          ☐ a. cats' behaviors.
                          ☐ b. cats' lives.
                          ☐ c. the cleanest animal.
                          ☐ d. facts about animals.   _____

Supporting   **3**   The cat cleans most of its body with its
Details   ☐ a. whiskers.
                          ☐ b. tongue.
                          ☐ c. paws.
                          ☐ d. face.   _____

Conclusion   **4**   From this passage, it appears that hair balls
                          ☐ a. make most cat owners angry.
                          ☐ b. can make a cat seriously ill.
                          ☐ c. are caused by the cat's whiskers.
                          ☐ d. happen only with adult cats.   _____

Clarifying   **5**   The author compares the tip of the cat's tongue
Devices   with a file in order to
                          ☐ a. make you think of your nails.
                          ☐ b. help you visualize its shape.
                          ☐ c. show how pointy it looks.
                          ☐ d. show how rough it is.   _____

Vocabulary   **6**   In this passage <u>glimmer</u> means
in Context   ☐ a. hint of light.
                          ☐ b. small shape.
                          ☐ c. bright shine.
                          ☐ d. glow.   _____

Add your scores for questions 1–6. Enter the total here   **Total**
and on the graph on page 211.   **Score**   _____

15 The Cat and the Minister

Here is a strange true story about a cat. A minister made a call on an elderly lady. He entered her house. She quickly said, "Please do not try to pet the cat. She's <u>nasty</u>. She'll give you a bad scratch." The minister replied, "Thanks for telling me. I won't try to pet her."

In the meantime, the cat crawled out from under the stove. She stretched. She looked at the visitor. She circled his chair. Then she jumped into his lap. She curled up and went to sleep. The lady gasped. She blurted, "She's never done that before. Not ever. My goodness. What has gotten into her?"

The half-hour visit was over. The minister stirred to leave. The cat nimbly and quietly leaped from his lap. She went right to the door. She meowed once and looked up at the minister. The minister opened the door. The cat walked out. She stopped. She looked over her shoulder at the minister. She meowed. Then she started across the lawn. She kept looking over her shoulder. The minister saw that she wanted him to follow. So he did. The cat led him to the far side of the house. It was shady there. She stopped in front of a low overhanging shrub. The cat meowed. She looked directly under the shrub. The minister crouched and knelt. Sure enough. There in the dark underside of the shrub was a nest of dry grass. Five kittens nestled there.

The mother cat meowed proudly. She looked up at her new friend. She arched her back. She rubbed her body against his legs. The minister bent over and stroked her silky fur. How did this all happen? No doubt it was cat sense. From the beginning the cat knew she had found a friend!

Main Idea	1	Answer	Score
	Mark the *main idea*	M	15
	Mark the statement that is *too broad*	B	5
	Mark the statement that is *too narrow*	N	5

a. The cat showed her kittens to the minister. ☐ _____

b. By watching and listening to cats we can better understand them. ☐ _____

c. A true story can teach us more about cats and whom they trust. ☐ _____

Score 15 points for each correct answer.   **Score**

Subject Matter 2 Another good title for this passage would be
- [ ] a. Cats and Kittens.
- [ ] b. The Minister Finds a Friend.
- [ ] c. Listening to Cats.
- [ ] d. More Cat Facts.   _____

Supporting Details 3 The mother cat kept her kittens
- [ ] a. in the basement of the house.
- [ ] b. in a dry grass nest.
- [ ] c. in a warm shoebox.
- [ ] d. in a bright part of the yard.   _____

Conclusion 4 The last paragraph suggests that
- [ ] a. cats can teach us a lot.
- [ ] b. there is more to learn about cat's behaviors.
- [ ] c. we can understand cats if we know how to listen to them.
- [ ] d. cat sense is like human sense.   _____

Clarifying Devices 5 To make his points about cats the author depends mainly on
- [ ] a. facts given by cat owners.
- [ ] b. details about cats and kittens.
- [ ] c. statements showing why everyone should own cats.
- [ ] d. a story about a cat.   _____

Vocabulary in Context 6 <u>Nasty</u> suggests that the cat was
- [ ] a. mean.
- [ ] b. dirty.
- [ ] c. angry.
- [ ] d. ugly.   _____

Add your scores for questions 1–6. Enter the total here and on the graph on page 211.   **Total Score**   _____

16 All About Chocolate

Do you like chocolate? Most people do. Some like it in bars. Others just like big squares of it. A box of it can be a great gift. Buy one for a friend. Give it as a surprise. See how happy that person gets.

Where does chocolate come from? It is made from cacao seeds. (The cacao is a small tree. It grows in the tropics.) Skins are removed from the seeds. The seeds are roasted. Then they are ground up. The taste at first is bitter. So sweeteners are added.

Say you just got a box of chocolate. Which piece do you pick first? A man has studied people's choices. He says they tell something about the person. Did you choose a round piece? You are a person who likes to party. Did you select an oval shape? You are a person who <u>strives</u>. You like to make things. You push your limits. Picking a square shape shows something else. This person is honest and truthful. You can depend on him or her.

What kind of chocolate do you pick? Maybe you like milk chocolate. This shows you have warm feelings about the past. Dark chocolate means something else. A person who chooses it looks toward the future. What about white chocolate? Would you choose it? If so, you may find it hard to make up your mind. Some people like chocolate with nuts. These are people who like to help others.

Do you believe these ideas? Can candy tell all these things? It doesn't really matter. There is one sure thing about eaters of chocolate. They eat it because they like it.

Main Idea	1		Answer	Score
	Mark the *main idea*		M	15
	Mark the statement that is *too broad*		B	5
	Mark the statement that is *too narrow*		N	5

a. The chocolate you choose can tell you something about yourself. ☐ _____

b. Chocolate comes from the cacao plant. ☐ _____

c. Almost everyone likes chocolate. ☐ _____

Score 15 points for each correct answer.   Score

2 This passage is mostly about
- ☐ a. the history of chocolate.
- ☐ b. why people like chocolate.
- ☐ c. why people choose certain shapes and types of chocolate.
- ☐ d. why chocolate will remain a popular treat in the future.

_____

Supporting Details **3** A liking of milk chocolate may show that a person
- ☐ a. looks forward to the future.
- ☐ b. thinks fondly of the past.
- ☐ c. enjoys parties and fun.
- ☐ d. has trouble making decisions.

_____

Conclusion **4** The last paragraph suggests that the writer
- ☐ a. believes all the information about chocolate.
- ☐ b. does not believe the information about chocolate.
- ☐ c. does not think it matters whether you believe the information or not.
- ☐ d. is trying to trick you into believing false information.

_____

Clarifying Devices **5** In the second paragraph, the author puts information in parentheses to
- ☐ a. tell more about the cacao tree.
- ☐ b. explain how chocolate is made.
- ☐ c. tell more about how cacao seeds are treated.
- ☐ d. give a short history of chocolate.

_____

Vocabulary in Context **6** In this passage <u>strives</u> means
- ☐ a. searches for better things.
- ☐ b. makes friends easily.
- ☐ c. loves the natural world.
- ☐ d. refuses to try at all.

_____

Add your scores for questions 1–6. Enter the total here and on the graph on page 211.   Total Score

_____

17 The Hard-Working Insect

Suppose a population count were made. Which insect would win out? You might think the fly or the mosquito. Neither right. The answer is the ant. Ants live in many places. (They are not at the North and South poles, though.) And they don't live alone. They live in colonies. Some colonies are as small as ten ants. Others have as many ants as there are people in New York City.

Ants may look alike. But they work differently. For instance, Harvester Ants gather seeds. They store them in their nests. If the seeds get damp, they spread them out in the sun to dry. These seeds are food for the long winter.

Honey Ants collect honeydew. Honeydew is a thin syrup. It drops from the stomachs of certain small insects. The ants store this honey in their nests. They use live ants as storage tanks. These ants just keep swallowing honey until they are as round as peas. When worker ants are hungry, they feed from the mouths of these honey-pots.

Then there are the Army Ants of Africa. They are hunters. They're fierce. They march in a column like soldiers. Nothing stops them. They even cross streams. They make a living bridge. Some ants <u>cling</u> to each other. The rest of the column marches over this bridge. They eat everything in their way. They eat insects, toads, and snakes. Anything!

Ants are well organized. But they cannot think. They follow a trail made by the front ants. If the trail goes in a circle, the whole column keeps going around. They circle till they all fall dead.

So what's the lesson? Work hard like an ant. But don't think like one!

Main Idea	1			
			Answer	**Score**
	Mark the *main idea*		M	15
	Mark the statement that is *too broad*		B	5
	Mark the statement that is *too narrow*		N	5

a. Ants have different jobs, but all are well organized and work hard. ☐ _____

b. The ant is a better worker than other insects. ☐ _____

c. Ants live in colonies of different sizes. ☐ _____

Score 15 points for each correct answer.   **Score**

Subject Matter   **2**   This passage deals mainly with the
- ☐ a. ants in Africa.
- ☐ b. things ants do.
- ☐ c. eating habits of ants.
- ☐ d. hardest working insect.   _____

Supporting Details   **3**   Honey ants are unusual because they
- ☐ a. march like soldiers.
- ☐ b. store honey in live ants.
- ☐ c. gather seeds.
- ☐ d. store seeds in their nests.   _____

Conclusion   **4**   To cross water, army ants
- ☐ a. walk around in circles.
- ☐ b. hold on to pieces of wood.
- ☐ c. get into fierce battles.
- ☐ d. climb over the backs of other ants.   _____

Clarifying Devices   **5**   To compare one ant's work habits to another, the author uses
- ☐ a. arguments.
- ☐ b. emotional appeals.
- ☐ c. examples.
- ☐ d. stories.   _____

Vocabulary in Context   **6**   The best definition for <u>cling</u> is
- ☐ a. hold on.
- ☐ b. cover.
- ☐ c. talk.
- ☐ d. bring food.   _____

Add your scores for questions 1–6. Enter the total here and on the graph on page 211.   **Total Score**   _____

18 Birds' Eggs

Birds' eggs come in a wide range of colors and markings. For example, the flicker's egg is pure white. In contrast, some ducks have solid black eggs. The eggs of the same species are almost always the same.

When held in the hand, the egg of a ground-nesting plover is easy to recognize. You feel that you could see it in any place. But not so fast. Put the plover's nested eggs in a field. Then try to find the eggs and nest. It's not so easy. Once a man was told to look along a straight plowed furrow. He was told that there were six nests with the eggs of plovers. He glued his eyes to the furrow and walked. When he reached the end of the furrow, he found one nest with eggs. He found this one because he stepped on it. It made him sad to have destroyed such a precious creation. But he did not step on the other five nests. He did not even see them. This story shows that birds know the art of blending.

Blending helps the species to survive. But it is not the only way to survival. Some eggs you can spot a mile away. Hearing this, most people will think that the blending <u>theory</u> does not work 100 percent. But wait! Something else happens. Bold-colored eggs have a foul taste. One cracked egg is enough. One small sip is too much. The snake will quickly glide away. The mongoose, too, will turn and trot off, spitting all the way. They learned the hard way. They will remember that bold color. The foul taste will be stored in their brain. They won't touch those bright eggs again. The rest of the eggs will hatch. The species will survive.

Main Idea	1		
		Answer	**Score**
	Mark the *main idea*	M	15
	Mark the statement that is *too broad*	B	5
	Mark the statement that is *too narrow*	N	5

a. Birds' eggs are very different, but all are protected by nature. ☐ _____

b. Eggs are nature's creation. ☐ _____

c. Birds' eggs are colored and patterned in each species. ☐ _____

Subject Matter   **2**   The best title for this passage is
- □ a. A Variety of Eggs.
- □ b. Nature's Course.
- □ c. Natural Protection for Eggs.
- □ d. A Wonder of an Egg.   _____

Supporting Details   **3**   The eggs of the plover
- □ a. stand out for their bright colors.
- □ b. fill farmer's fields.
- □ c. blend into their surroundings.
- □ d. make farmers sad.   _____

Conclusion   **4**   We can conclude from the passage that
- □ a. the designs on some eggs help to conceal them.
- □ b. very few eggs have a specific pattern.
- □ c. farmers notice eggs with patterns.
- □ d. each design is unique with each egg.   _____

Clarifying Devices   **5**   The author develops the main idea by means of
- □ a. examples and proof.
- □ b. comparison and contrast.
- □ c. one long story.
- □ d. carefully chosen adjectives and adverbs.   _____

Vocabulary in Context   **6**   As used in this passage, <u>theory</u> seems to mean
- □ a. personal opinions.
- □ b. unproved idea.
- □ c. stated fact.
- □ d. pattern.   _____

Add your scores for questions 1–6. Enter the total here and on the graph on page 211.   **Total Score**   _____

19 A Stack of Pancakes

You are on a trip. You stop for breakfast. You order a stack of pancakes and perhaps coffee. The pancakes and coffee are placed before you. Now, the question. What two other items naturally come with the meal? If you said, "Maple syrup and butter," you are right. You pick up the small bottle of syrup. There's print on it. It tells where the syrup came from. It might be one of three places: Quebec, New York, or Vermont. Quebec is the leader in maple syrup. It produces about 1¹/₂ million gallons a year. New York and Vermont produce far less.

The syrup comes from maple trees. It comes from black, silver, and red maples. The largest amounts come from the sugar-maple tree. The process starts in early spring. A hole is bored into the tree trunk. It's about three inches deep. The hole must be deep enough to tap the sapwood. Next a spout is <u>inserted</u>. It is the runway for the dripping sap. The right size is important. It must be watertight. Pails are then hung on the spout. Sometimes strong plastic bags are hung instead. The pails or bags are covered. This keeps out the rain, leaves, and bark.

Each day, sap is collected. It is poured into tanks. These tanks are on sleds if there is snow. Otherwise tanks are on wheeled carts. The sap then goes to the saphouse. Here it is boiled. Most of the water is boiled away as steam. But not all the water. Some water is left. If all were steamed away, what would you have? The answer is hard sugar. The object, of course, is to have syrup. So you leave just the right amount of water.

The right balance gives you a tasty syrup. Not too thick. Not too thin. But just right.

Main Idea	1	Answer	Score
	Mark the *main idea*	M	15
	Mark the statement that is *too broad*	B	5
	Mark the statement that is *too narrow*	N	5

a. Making syrup is an involved process that begins with maple trees. ☐ ____

b. Most syrup comes from sugar-maple trees. ☐ ____

c. Maple syrup comes from various places. ☐ ____

Score 15 points for each correct answer.   Score

Subject Matter   2   The passage is mostly about
- [ ] a. pancakes.
- [ ] b. maple syrup.
- [ ] c. breakfast.
- [ ] d. maple trees.   _____

Supporting   3   According to the passage, one step in making
Details   syrup is to
- [ ] a. begin in early summer.
- [ ] b. collect water in pails.
- [ ] c. collect sap at the top of the tree.
- [ ] d. boil the sap.   _____

Conclusion   4   One can conclude from the last paragraph
- [ ] a. the right amount of water and sap make a
      good syrup.
- [ ] b. syrup is best on pancakes at breakfast.
- [ ] c. adding water to hard sugar makes the best
      syrup.
- [ ] d. the author has made syrup before.   _____

Clarifying   5   The author begins the passage by
Devices
- [ ] a. listing steps in a process.
- [ ] b. using a personal experience.
- [ ] c. encouraging us to imagine.
- [ ] d. describing a trip to Vermont.   _____

Vocabulary   6   Inserted means
in Context
- [ ] a. removed.
- [ ] b. dug into.
- [ ] c. put in.
- [ ] d. purchased.   _____

Add your scores for questions 1–6. Enter the total here   Total
and on the graph on page 211.   Score   _____

20 Androcles and the Lion

This happened in the first century A.D. Androcles was a slave to a cruel master. The master's ship stopped for water on the west coast of Africa. Androcles escaped. He crawled into a small cave. He hid there. Suddenly the cave entrance darkened. It was a large lion. The lion did not rush. Instead, it limped slowly. The lion's head was low. Its eyes were dull. Its fur looked matted. Exhausted, the lion stretched out beside Androcles. Androcles saw the swollen paw. The chewed end of a huge thorn stuck out. The lion must have been in pain for many days.

Androcles knew the African thorn was barbed. The barb was like that of a fishhook. If it was pulled, flesh would tear too. The pain would be great. Androcles leaned over the lion. He stroked its mane. The lion licked Androcles' hand. It seemed to understand. There would be pain.

Androcles sat down. He put his feet against the lion's body for <u>leverage</u>. He grasped the thorn tightly with both hands. Then he jerked quickly and powerfully. The barb was clutched in his hands. Yes, some flesh hung off the barb. He quickly looked. A stream of bad blood and yellow infection spurted out of the paw. The infection had gone up the lion's leg.

Androcles gently squeezed the leg to drain it. The lion lay as if dead. Androcles seized a broken coconut shell. He filled the shell in a stream. He carried the water back to the lion. The lion lifted its head. It first licked Androcles' hand. Then it lapped all the water.

Androcles ran for a refill. He never came back. As he bent for more water, hands suddenly gripped him. The ship's crew tied him up. They dragged him away. He was a slave again.

Main Idea   1

	Answer	Score
Mark the *main idea*	M	15
Mark the statement that is *too broad*	B	5
Mark the statement that is *too narrow*	N	5

a. Androcles' tenderness and bravery saved a hurt lion. ☐ _____

b. People who are kind and resourceful can cure sick lions. ☐ _____

c. Androcles removed a thorn from the lion's paw. ☐ _____

Score 15 points for each correct answer.   Score

Subject Matter   **2**   This passage is about
- ☐ a. Androcles' life as a slave.
- ☐ b. how to save a lion.
- ☐ c. how Androcles hid from his slave master.
- ☐ d. Androcles' kind act.

_____

Supporting Details   **3**   One way Androcles helped the lion was by
- ☐ a. getting the infection out of its leg.
- ☐ b. feeding it fish from a stream.
- ☐ c. wrapping its paw in a bandage.
- ☐ d. washing its leg with water.

_____

Conclusion   **4**   We may conclude that
- ☐ a. Androcles was the first slave to escape a slave ship.
- ☐ b. Androcles was sold because his master did not want him to escape again.
- ☐ c. if Androcles had not helped the lion he may have escaped.
- ☐ d. if the lion had healed it would have stayed with Androcles.

_____

Clarifying Devices   **5**   This passage can be best described as a
- ☐ a. descriptive essay.
- ☐ b. story.
- ☐ c. piece of nonfiction.
- ☐ d. joke.

_____

Vocabulary in Context   **6**   The word <u>leverage</u> is closest in meaning to
- ☐ a. balance.
- ☐ b. action.
- ☐ c. support.
- ☐ d. power.

_____

Add your scores for questions 1–6. Enter the total here and on the graph on page 211.   Total Score   _____

21 Where Are All the Buffalo?

American Indians of the past hunted buffalo. They did not use guns. They used bow and arrow. They rode full speed on ponies. They went bareback. They covered the rough prairie. Sometimes horses stumbled. This could mean disaster. The thousand pounding hooves never stopped.

How big is a buffalo bull? Some weigh 3,000 pounds. The average is about 2,000 pounds. The bull is about six feet at the shoulders. It is 10 to 12 feet long. That's from the tip of its nose to the end of its tail. From horn tip to horn tip is about three feet.

The buffalo was life to the Indian. It was meat for the summer's pot. Strips dried in the sun were winter food. Hides made strong tepees. They gave shelter from rains and snows. They made a warm home.

Just think. As recently as 1850, there were 20 million buffalo. They covered the Western plains. By 1889, there were 500. The needless killing! Not by Indians. But by "sportsmen" safely shooting from railroad cars. The buffalo that remained were gathered up. They're in preserves now. There are about 10,000 in the United States. They are mainly around Yellowstone. There are 15,000 in Canada. Near Great Slave Lake is home for most.

Buffalo like company. They live and <u>thrive</u> in herds. They are full grown in eight years. Some live 30 to 40 years. They feed mostly on grass. So the prairie is just right for them. Tame them? Ranchers tried. All failed. Buffalo have quick tempers.

One thing is true. They were the "cattle" of the American Indian.

Main Idea	1	Answer	Score
	Mark the *main idea*	M	15
	Mark the statement that is *too broad*	B	5
	Mark the statement that is *too narrow*	N	5

a. Buffalo hunting is not as easy as one would think. ☐ _____

b. The buffalo, a vital part of American Indian life, is much scarcer now than in the past. ☐ _____

c. American Indian buffalo hunters used bow and arrow. ☐ _____

Subject Matter   **2**   The main subject of this passage is
    ☐ a. hunting.
    ☐ b. how American Indians of the past lived.
    ☐ c. where buffalo live today.
    ☐ d. the buffalo.   _____

Supporting Details   **3**   The buffalo was life to the Indians because it
    ☐ a. provided food, clothing, and shelter.
    ☐ b. was part of their favorite sport.
    ☐ c. made them strong hunters.
    ☐ d. lived as long as they did.   _____

Conclusion   **4**   The writer implies that
    ☐ a. Indians wasted many parts of the buffalo.
    ☐ b. buffalo became endangered because of
        white civilians.
    ☐ c. hunting is easier when bow and arrow are
        used.
    ☐ d. although buffalo are big they are very calm
        and gentle.   _____

Clarifying Devices   **5**   The writer puts quotation marks around the
word "sportsmen" to
    ☐ a. show that these men were important.
    ☐ b. state a fact.
    ☐ c. suggest that buffalo hunting was a sporting
        activity.
    ☐ d. suggest the writer's opinion about what these
        men were doing.   _____

Vocabulary in Context   **6**   <u>Thrive</u> most closely means
    ☐ a. fight.
    ☐ b. do well.
    ☐ c. do poorly.
    ☐ d. grow.   _____

Add your scores for questions 1–6. Enter the total here   **Total**
and on the graph on page 211.   **Score**   _____

22 The Eskimos' Kitchen

Where did the name *Eskimo* come from? It comes from an American Indian word. It means eaters of raw meat. Eskimos have always eaten raw meat. They liked the flavor. That is one reason they did it. But there is another reason. It may be the real one. Early Eskimos had little or no wood. They could not build big fires. They did have oil made from whale blubber. This oil was used mainly for lamps. Cooking with a lamp has a <u>drawback</u>. It takes a long time.

Eskimos lived mainly on seal and caribou meat. They also ate a lot of fish. Meat came from birds, musk oxen, and polar bears. Once in a while there was whale. Eggs were part of the diet too. They also gathered a few wild plants. The season was short. Not much grew. They got vegetables from the caribou. How did they do this? It was simple. They ate the undigested contents of a caribou's stomach. The contents were vegetable matter.

Early Eskimos did not have iron pots. They cooked in pots made from soft rock. This rock was called soapstone. They made lamps from this rock too.

Eskimos ate several small meals a day. These were eaten on plates. The plates were made of wood. Wood was scarce. But when Eskimos went to hunt in the south, they would bring back wood. They also had forks. These were made of bone. There was always plenty of bone from the animals. Drinking cups were made from the horns of musk oxen. The women also used a special knife. It is called a ulu. It is used in the kitchen. It is shaped like a half moon. Ulus were made of various things. Sometimes they were made of horn. Sometimes bone was used.

Main Idea	1		
		Answer	Score
	Mark the *main idea*	M	15
	Mark the statement that is *too broad*	B	5
	Mark the statement that is *too narrow*	N	5

a. Eskimos' food and eating utensils came from animals and simple materials. ☐ ____

b. The Eskimos had many uses for animals. ☐ ____

c. Meat was the Eskimos' main diet, eaten in many small meals a day. ☐ ____

Subject Matter 2 This passage deals with
- [ ] a. raw meat.
- [ ] b. meat eaters.
- [ ] c. Eskimos.
- [ ] d. kitchens.

_____

Supporting Details 3 Why did Eskimos use bones for forks?
- [ ] a. They had sharp edges.
- [ ] b. It was better than metal.
- [ ] c. Bones were hard and strong.
- [ ] d. There was a lot of bone around.

_____

Conclusion 4 This passage indicated that Eskimos
- [ ] a. were clever in using available materials.
- [ ] b. did not like vegetables.
- [ ] c. had trouble finding food.
- [ ] d. are similar to American Indians.

_____

Clarifying Devices 5 In the first paragraph, the word *but* indicates
- [ ] a. that a definition will follow.
- [ ] b. a contradiction or contrast.
- [ ] c. an example.
- [ ] d. the time something happened.

_____

Vocabulary in Context 6 In this passage, the word <u>drawback</u> means
- [ ] a. advantage.
- [ ] b. ways to do something.
- [ ] c. forms.
- [ ] d. disadvantage.

_____

Add your scores for questions 1–6. Enter the total here and on the graph on page 211. **Total Score**

_____

23 A Tasty Weed

Finding a meal in a field used to be common. Years ago many people in this country had just come from Europe. They brought old customs with them. And they knew their plants. Often you would seeing people cutting in a field. They had a bag in one hand. They had a knife in the other. What were they doing? Maybe this will surprise you. They were cutting dandelions.

The dandelion is one of the most <u>maligned</u> of weeds. It is really a living supermarket. The leaves of the young plant are delicious in salads. The leaves can also be cooked. With beans they make a hearty meal.

Dandelion wine can also be made. The blossoms must be picked in the daylight. Here is why. The blossoms close at night. They do not open until the sun comes up.

All parts of the plant can be used. Roots and leaves are used in medicines. Sometimes the juice is squeezed out. Other times the dry root is ground into powder. There is enough root to do it both ways. The root often grows more than three feet long. It grows best in soft, rich, sandy soil.

There is also a way to play with dandelions. When ripe, the blossoms form a soft white head. At the bottom of each white strand clings a tiny seed. Children pick the flower. They hold it by the stem. Then they blow hard at the white head. The soft white strands float off. They are carried by the wind into the world.

The dandelion was brought here from Europe. The early colonists brought it. They knew they would find a use for it here.

Main Idea	1		
		Answer	Score
	Mark the *main idea*	M	15
	Mark the statement that is *too broad*	B	5
	Mark the statement that is *too narrow*	N	5

a. Most often the dandelion is used in salads. ☐ _____

b. The dandelion is useful in many ways. ☐ _____

c. Weeds can be tasty. ☐ _____

Score 15 points for each correct answer.   **Score**

Subject Matter   **2**   This passage is primarily about
    ☐ a. tasty plants.
    ☐ b. using dandelions.
    ☐ c. dandelion wine.
    ☐ d. eating weeds.   ____

Supporting Details   **3**   The dandelion is called a living supermarket because it
    ☐ a. grows in combination with other weeds.
    ☐ b. is grown on large farms.
    ☐ c. can be sold for high prices in stores.
    ☐ d. has many possible uses.   ____

Conclusion   **4**   From the passage, you can conclude that the dandelion is
    ☐ a. better tasting than most vegetables.
    ☐ b. not fatal if eaten.
    ☐ c. something that can be bought in supermarkets.
    ☐ d. more nutritious than most weeds.   ____

Clarifying Devices   **5**   The author gives the reader a good understanding of the dandelion through the use of
    ☐ a. detailed comparisons.
    ☐ b. good examples.
    ☐ c. personal opinions.
    ☐ d. complex reasoning.   ____

Vocabulary in Context   **6**   The word <u>maligned</u>, as used in this passage, means
    ☐ a. spoken badly of.
    ☐ b. tasty.
    ☐ c. cheaply grown.
    ☐ d. constantly destroyed.   ____

Add your scores for questions 1–6. Enter the total here and on the graph on page 211.   **Total Score**   ____

47

24 The Apple and Apple Cider

The apple tree has been around for a long time. Early humans picked apples for food. Today the apple is still the most valuable fruit crop. It is more valuable than the orange. Peach, pear, and plum crops are valuable. But the apple is worth all of them combined.

Apple trees grow just about everywhere. But they do not grow in very hot or very cold places. Apples are a big crop. The world's crop is almost a billion bushels a year. About one fourth of that is used for juice. How much juice comes from an apple? A lot! A fresh raw apple is about 84 percent water. But it is thick water. The water is full of fruit sugar.

The juice is made into cider. No two batches are the same. Why? Because cider makers mix different kinds of apples. This brings out a <u>unique</u> flavor. For example, the Red Delicious is sweet. The Ida Red is tart. But mixing them makes a great drink. Not too sweet. Not too tart. There are over 7,500 different kinds of apples. So makers have a big choice.

Let's watch the making of cider. Here is what you see. First, the apples are washed. Then they go on a moving belt. There they are sorted. The bad apples are picked out. The good stay. These are fed into a grinder. The grinder grinds them to a pulp. The pulp is called *cheese*. The cheese is placed in cloth bags. The bags are stacked on the floor of the press. Then the press slowly winds down. The cheese-filled bags are squeezed hard. The juice flows down between the bottom slats. The base is like a tub. It holds the cider.

The cheese must be removed at once. If it isn't, every wasp within miles will come after it.

Main Idea	1		
		Answer	Score
Mark the *main idea*		M	15
Mark the statement that is *too broad*		B	5
Mark the statement that is *too narrow*		N	5
a. The apple crop is more important than the orange crop.		☐	_____
b. The apple is valuable as a fruit and as cider.		☐	_____
c. Apples are useful.		☐	_____

Score 15 points for each correct answer.

Subject Matter   **2**   This selection is mostly about
- ☐ a. the history of apples.
- ☐ b. the variety of types of apples.
- ☐ c. picking apples.
- ☐ d. making cider.   _____

Supporting   **3**   The squeezed pulp is
Details
- ☐ a. made into apple sauce.
- ☐ b. used in baking.
- ☐ c. thrown out.
- ☐ d. squeezed a second time.   _____

Conclusion   **4**   The passages indicates that
- ☐ a. apples can be used in more ways than one.
- ☐ b. cider makers can only use one type of apple.
- ☐ c. the apple crop is mainly used for juice.
- ☐ d. making cider is very time consuming.   _____

Clarifying   **5**   The author explains making cider through
Devices
- ☐ a. a series of images.
- ☐ b. a description of the process.
- ☐ c. an explanation of its history.
- ☐ d. a set of examples.   _____

Vocabulary   **6**   In this passage <u>unique</u> means
in Context
- ☐ a. strange.
- ☐ b. special or unusual.
- ☐ c. tasty.
- ☐ d. sour.   _____

Add your scores for questions 1–6. Enter the total here   **Total**
and on the graph on page 211.   **Score**   _____

25 The Pied Piper of Hamelin

Some say this event took place in the town of Hamelin. This town is in Germany. (It is now spelled Hameln.) The town was infested by rats. The rats ate the grain in the fields. They ate the grain in the storehouses. They ate the food in people's homes. Some rats were so large that cats were afraid of them. People feared the spread of disease. They were <u>desperate</u>.

One day a man appeared in town. He was dressed in a suit of many colors. He listened to the problem. He offered to rid the town of the rats. "All of them," he said. The people gasped at the promise. How happy they would be if it could be done. The mayor wanted to know the price. The man stated a sum of money. The mayor agreed. The people cheered. Could he really carry out his promise? The mayor asked when he could start. The man said, "Right now."

Here is what he did. He drew out his pipe. He tested it with a few notes. Then he walked along the streets. He played a haunting tune. The people lined the sidewalks. Everyone was watching. What they saw amazed them. With the first note, noises from the cellars and gutters were heard. Then hordes of rats came scrambling into the street. The road was just solid with rats. Gray ones, black ones, young ones, and old ones. They followed the piper. The tune was magical. It was like an unseen magnet. The air was filled with squeals and the swish of little feet.

The Piper never looked back. He headed for the Weser River. He kept piping, and the rats followed him. He stepped into a small rowboat and gently pushed off. The rats plunged after him into the water. They tried to swim but went under. The slow current floated them down stream.

Main Idea	1			
			Answer	**Score**
	Mark the *main idea*		M	15
	Mark the statement that is *too broad*		B	5
	Mark the statement that is *too narrow*		N	5

a. The Pied Piper is a famous story that has some truth to it. ☐ _____

b. The rats came out of the cellars and gutters. ☐ _____

c. The Pied Piper led the rats out of town with his strange tune. ☐ _____

Subject Matter   **2**   This passage is mainly about
- ☐ a. stories that are both true and untrue.
- ☐ b. the Pied Piper's tune.
- ☐ c. the story of the Pied Piper.
- ☐ d. Hamelin's rat problem.

     _____

Supporting Details   **3**   To get the rats to follow him the Pied Piper
- ☐ a. played his pipe.
- ☐ b. led them to water.
- ☐ c. used magic.
- ☐ d. walked through the streets shouting.

     _____

Conclusion   **4**   People may believe the story is true because
- ☐ a. rats cannot swim.
- ☐ b. Hamelin is a real place.
- ☐ c. the rats were gone one day.
- ☐ d. it has been told for hundreds of years.

     _____

Clarifying Devices   **5**   The writer tells the story by
- ☐ a. using facts and details from history.
- ☐ b. asking questions and then giving answers.
- ☐ c. first setting the scene, then describing the action.
- ☐ d. using a number of examples.

     _____

Vocabulary in Context   **6**   In this passage <u>desperate</u> means
- ☐ a. without hope.
- ☐ b. angry.
- ☐ c. tired.
- ☐ d. strong willed.

     _____

Add your scores for questions 1–6. Enter the total here and on the graph on page 211.   **Total Score**   _____

26 The Children of Hamelin

The piper freed the town of Hamelin. He played his pipe. The rats followed him out of town. So he spoke to the mayor. "I've done what I've promised. Now pay me." The mayor said, "The work was too easy. You deserve no money." The people hung their heads but said nothing.

The piper took out his pipe again. This time he played a different tune. It was a strange melody. All of a sudden came the sound of running feet. The children ran from the sidewalks. They ran from their homes. They scrambled with laughter and joy. They followed the Piper. Mothers cried out to come back. But the music had magic in it. The happy children followed. They followed the Piper to the Köppen Hill. There the Piper led them into a cave. When the last child ran through, the cave closed like a door. The parents cried out. They beat on the stone door. They ran around hysterically. It was to no <u>avail</u>. The children were never seen again.

The children were gone. This is a fact. In the present town of Hamelin are more facts. On the wall of some old houses is a record. The record speaks of July 26, 1284. It says that a Piper led 130 children out of town. They were lost in Köppen Hill.

The Pied Piper may be fiction—a legend. But wrapped in the legend are facts. The town probably did lose 130 children. But they lost them in another way. The way was probably this. The nearby land of Moravia was thinly settled. Agents from there probably promised free land to the young. The young people left. The old folks stayed. The net result was this. The people of Hamelin lost their children. Not to the cave in Köppen Hill, but to the land of Moravia.

Main Idea	1	Answer	Score
	Mark the *main idea*	M	15
	Mark the statement that is *too broad*	B	5
	Mark the statement that is *too narrow*	N	5

a. The Pied Piper story is made up of both true events and fictional ones. ☐ _____

b. A legend is both factual and fictional. ☐ _____

c. The piper led children to a cave where they were never seen again. ☐ _____

Score 15 points for each correct answer.   **Score**

Subject Matter   **2**   The best alternate title for this passage would be
- ☐ a. The Unhappy Townspeople.
- ☐ b. The Pied Piper: Fact and Fiction.
- ☐ c. The Piper Steals Children.
- ☐ d. Moravian Migration.

_____

Supporting Details   **3**   The Pied Piper led the children out of town because he
- ☐ a. did not like children.
- ☐ b. took them to free land.
- ☐ c. was angry about not being paid.
- ☐ d. needed them to work for him.

_____

Conclusion   **4**   The writer implies in the last paragraph that
- ☐ a. sad stories can be more interesting than happy ones.
- ☐ b. losing children is sad no matter how it happens.
- ☐ c. legends are often based on true events.
- ☐ d. we should not believe everything we hear.

_____

Clarifying Devices   **5**   The author uses the simile "the cave closed like a door" to
- ☐ a. show the reader why the door closed.
- ☐ b. help the reader imagine how the closed-up cave entrance looked.
- ☐ c. get the reader to think about the cave.
- ☐ d. describe why the children could not open the door.

_____

Vocabulary in Context   **6**   Another word for <u>avail</u> might be
- ☐ a. answer.
- ☐ b. place.
- ☐ c. help.
- ☐ d. openings.

_____

Add your scores for questions 1–6. Enter the total here and on the graph on page 212.   **Total Score**

_____

27 Acres of Diamonds

Did you ever hear of Russell H. Conwell? Few people have. Even fewer know what he did. Conwell founded Temple University. He was not a wealthy man. Then how did he found a University? It's better to start at the beginning. Here is the story.

Conwell was a minister. He worked in Philadelphia. A young man came to him for advice. He wanted to be a minister. Conwell offered to teach him Latin. He would do it one night a week. The young man asked to bring some friends along. Conwell said, "Bring as many as you wish." The young man brought seven. The lessons began in Conwell's office. Soon they moved to a large room. Then it was a building. Then two buildings. After four years the group had grown to 590 students. At this point, a college charter was secured.

Money was now needed. Conwell went on a lecture tour. Here is why he was prepared for it. At a reunion of his old Civil War comrades, he had given a talk. It was a huge success. Others <u>clamored</u> to hear it. He went on a tour and gave his talk. In fact, he delivered the same lecture over 6,000 times. The lecture earned over seven million dollars. At that time, this was a very great sum. Each time, the money went to the school.

What was the famous lecture about? Its title was "Acres of Diamonds." It was about a man who searched for diamonds. He searched far and wide. Then he found what he was looking for. It was in his own backyard. The moral was this. Your wealth is where you are. But you have to dig for it. You must dig and believe. If you do, you'll find success right where you are.

Main Idea	1		
		Answer	**Score**
	Mark the *main idea*	M	15
	Mark the statement that is *too broad*	B	5
	Mark the statement that is *too narrow*	N	5

a. Founding a university takes time, money, and dedication. ☐ _____

b. Russell H. Conwell founded Temple University and funded it through lectures. ☐ _____

c. Russell H. Conwell gave a speech called "Acres of Diamonds." ☐ _____

Score 15 points for each correct answer.   **Score**

Subject Matter **2** This passage mostly deals with
    ☐ a. founding Temple University.
    ☐ b. diamonds.
    ☐ c. Conwell's students.
    ☐ d. Conwell's fame.   _____

Supporting Details **3** To raise money for the school, Conwell
    ☐ a. taught classes.
    ☐ b. lectured at Temple.
    ☐ c. went on a lecture tour.
    ☐ d. sold diamonds.   _____

Conclusion **4** We can conclude from the passage that Conwell
    ☐ a. was a very good and interesting speaker.
    ☐ b. visited Turkey.
    ☐ c. lectured only to the rich.
    ☐ d. was not popular with his students.   _____

Clarifying Devices **5** The author develops the main idea by
    ☐ a. recalling people's descriptions.
    ☐ b. telling a true story.
    ☐ c. explaining how something works.
    ☐ d. listing events.   _____

Vocabulary in Context **6** The best definition for <u>clamored</u> in this passage is
    ☐ a. demanded noisily.
    ☐ b. ran quickly.
    ☐ c. asked politely.
    ☐ d. came.   _____

Add your scores for questions 1–6. Enter the total here **Total**
and on the graph on page 212. **Score** _____

28 Looking for Diamonds

Here is the story of the man who sought diamonds. Near the Indus River lived a farmer. He had rich lands. He owned orchards, grain fields, and gardens. He was a happy, wealthy man. One day this farmer was visited by an old monk. The monk sat by the fire. He told the farmer how the world was formed. He told how granite was made. He ended by saying, "The diamond is the most precious of all substances. It is a congealed drop of sunlight."

The farmer, Ali Hafed, was spellbound. Then the old monk said this. "If you have a handful of diamonds you can buy a whole country." To emphasize the value, he said more. He said that with a diamond mine Ali Hafed could make his children into rulers.

Ali Hafed could not get the thought of diamonds out of his mind. He kept thinking, "I want a mine of diamonds." The next morning he went to the monk's house. He asked, "Where can I find diamonds?" The monk said, "First find a river. It must run over white sands. The river must be between high mountains. In the white sands, you'll find diamonds."

Ali Hafed sold his farm. He put his money in a bank. He left his family in the care of friends. He went in search of diamonds. He roamed and roamed. He followed stories. Finally he was footsore and weary. Years had passed. His strength was gone. Finally all his wealth was gone too. He stood at the shore of a great sea. A great wave came rolling in. He threw his weary body into it. He sank beneath the wave. He was discouraged and old. His family was far away. He died a sad and weary pauper.

Main Idea	1		
		Answer	**Score**
	Mark the *main idea*	M	15
	Mark the statement that is *too broad*	B	5
	Mark the statement that is *too narrow*	N	5
	a. Ali Hafed gave up a comfortable life to search for diamonds.	☐	_____
	b. Some people are never satisfied with what they have.	☐	_____
	c. The old monk told Ali Hafed where to search for diamonds.	☐	_____

Subject Matter **2** Another good title for this passage would be
- ☐ a. Ali Hafed and the Monk.
- ☐ b. A Way to Be Wealthy.
- ☐ c. From Riches to Rags.
- ☐ d. Death Near the Sea.

_____

Supporting Details **3** The old monk told Hafed he would find diamonds
- ☐ a. near his own house.
- ☐ b. by the ocean.
- ☐ c. in a river.
- ☐ d. beside a field.

_____

Conclusion **4** From this passage we can conclude that
- ☐ a. the old monk knew Ali Hafed would not return.
- ☐ b. Ali felt money was more important than his family or friends.
- ☐ c. the old monk planned to trick Ali Hafed.
- ☐ d. Ali Hafed was not happy at home.

_____

Clarifying Devices **5** The author uses quotes in this story to
- ☐ a. show an exact knowledge of what the characters said.
- ☐ b. make the story sound more interesting.
- ☐ c. introduce difficult words.
- ☐ d. show that time is passing.

_____

Vocabulary in Context **6** In this passage a <u>pauper</u> is a
- ☐ a. salesman.
- ☐ b. beggar.
- ☐ c. old man.
- ☐ d. farmer.

_____

Add your scores for questions 1–6. Enter the total here and on the graph on page 212.   **Total Score**   _____

29 The Grass Is Greener

The story of the man who sought diamonds continues. Let us go back to Ali Hafed's old farm. The man who bought it was glad a stream ran through the farm. It provided cool water. One day the man led his camel there to drink. The camel put its nose into the clear water. Then the man noticed a curious flash of light. He put his hand into the white sands and pulled out a black stone. It had an eye of light that flashed. He took the stone into the house. He placed it on the mantel. It was just a pretty pebble. He forgot about it.

The same old monk came to meet the new owner. The men visited for a while. Then the monk saw the flash of light from the mantel. He rushed up and said, "This is a diamond. Has Ali Hafed returned?"

"No, Ali Hafed has not returned," replied the farmer. "Anyway, that's just a stone. I found it right out here in the stream." The monk replied, "I know a diamond when I see one. This is a diamond."

The two men rushed to the stream. They stirred the white sands. Their fingers brought up stones more beautiful than the first. The site at that stream became a famous one. It was the home of the great diamond mines of Golconda. The diamonds from this mine grace <u>regal</u> crowns. One is part of the crown jewels of England. Another, the largest diamond on earth, is part of Russia's crown jewels.

The stones were right in Ali Hafed's backyard. He could have stayed home and found them.

Main Idea	1	Answer	Score
	Mark the *main idea*	M	15
	Mark the statement that is *too broad*	B	5
	Mark the statement that is *too narrow*	N	5

a. The farmer discovered a diamond but didn't know what it was. ☐ _____

b. Ali Hafed could have discovered many diamonds on his own property. ☐ _____

c. To believe in yourself is the greatest lesson people can learn. ☐ _____

Subject Matter   **2**   This passage is about
- ☐ a. finding diamonds.
- ☐ b. a foolish monk.
- ☐ c. the Russian crown jewels.
- ☐ d. a camel that spotted a diamond.   _____

Supporting Details   **3**   Golconda is
- ☐ a. the most expensive diamond found in the stream.
- ☐ b. the name of Ali Hafed's farm.
- ☐ c. a museum that exhibits diamonds.
- ☐ d. a famous diamond mine.   _____

Conclusion   **4**   In the last paragraph the writer implies that people
- ☐ a. are only greedy because they are foolish.
- ☐ b. can find diamonds in their own yards.
- ☐ c. must look for success within themselves.
- ☐ d. should not want riches.   _____

Clarifying Devices   **5**   In the first paragraph, the writer calls the stone a "pebble" to show that
- ☐ a. it was worthless.
- ☐ b. it was small.
- ☐ c. it looked black.
- ☐ d. the farmer did not recognize its worth.   _____

Vocabulary in Context   **6**   Regal means
- ☐ a. beautiful.
- ☐ b. gold.
- ☐ c. royal.
- ☐ d. expensive.   _____

Add your scores for questions 1–6. Enter the total here and on the graph on page 212.   Total Score   _____

30 Swarming Locusts

Is a locust the same as a grasshopper? If you said yes you are right. Locusts are about two inches long. They have large heads, four wings, and two large eyes. Each locust weighs about two grams.

How can you tell when locusts are around? Their <u>droning</u> sound gives them away. They have no vocal cords. They make sound this way. They rub their hind legs on their front wings. This rubbing causes their wings to vibrate. The action is somewhat like playing a violin.

By itself, a locust is practically harmless. But in a swarm, watch out. Locusts are very destructive. There are two reasons for this. First, each locust, pound for pound, eats 60 to 100 times as much as a human being. One million locusts each day eat as much as 20 elephants or 500 people. Second, a moving swarm may carpet the ground almost solidly. There may be 30 to 60 locusts per square yard. One swarm near the Red Sea covered 2,000 square miles. That's almost the size of the entire state of Delaware.

Locust swarms are like a cloud. They can block out the light of the sun. Railroad trains have been stopped by them. Swarms have covered tracks for miles. Soon their crushed bodies made the tracks too slippery. The train wheels just spun around. There was no traction. Swarms on roads are even worse. Try driving over one. It is similar to driving a car on solid ice.

Locusts fly with great speed, and their endurance is amazing. Swarms have been seen as much as 1,200 miles from land. These swarms are doomed. They tire and drop into the water. There they make rich food for fish. One swarm that started from West Africa did reach England.

Main Idea	1		
		Answer	**Score**
Mark the *main idea*		M	15
Mark the statement that is *too broad*		B	5
Mark the statement that is *too narrow*		N	5

a. Locusts can be very destructive in swarms. ☐ _____

b. Locusts eat as much as twenty elephants. ☐ _____

c. Some insects can be harmful when in a group. ☐ _____

Subject Matter   **2**   This passage is mainly concerned with
☐ a. the destructive ability of locusts.
☐ b. the harmlessness of individual locusts.
☐ c. controlling the locust population.
☐ d. the importance of locusts to humans.   _____

Supporting   **3**   A locust
Details
☐ a. can eat its own weight every day.
☐ b. always travels in swarms.
☐ c. can fly over long distances.
☐ d. is no larger than a kernel of corn.   _____

Conclusion   **4**   The destructiveness of swarms of locust results
from all of the following except
☐ a. the swarm's huge appetite.
☐ b. the large area covered by a swarm.
☐ c. the large number of locusts in a swarm.
☐ d. the extreme weight of a locust swarm.   _____

Clarifying   **5**   The author uses the simile "Locust swarms are
Devices   like a cloud" to
☐ a. show the way words can be used to explain.
☐ b. get the reader to understand his opinion.
☐ c. help the reader imagine how locusts look.
☐ d. persuade the reader to become interested
        in locusts.   _____

Vocabulary   **6**   Another word for <u>droning</u> might be
in Context
☐ a. humming.
☐ b. playing.
☐ c. knocking.
☐ d. clicking.   _____

Add your scores for questions 1–6. Enter the total here   **Total**
and on the graph on page 212.   **Score**   _____

31 A Face-Off in the Colosseum

The Colosseum is in Rome. It is now in ruins, but once it was a great arena. It looked like our football stadiums. It could seat about 45,000 people. It was mainly used to watch gladiators fight. Most gladiators were prisoners of war. They were made to fight with swords and other weapons. They fought until one was killed. Then the winner was set free.

The Colosseum was also used for another spectacle. An unarmed man would be thrown into the arena. A hungry wild lion would be released, and the spectators would watch the man being torn and eaten. Here's an account of one such event.

The cage was opened. A starved, almost crazed lion sprang forth. The prey was in the center. The man stood with only a rock in one hand. In the other was a fistful of sand. That's all he had. The lion never paused. It made long and powerful <u>bounds</u>. With each leap, its claws set forth showers of sand.

The stands were silent. People held their breaths. With one more leap, the lion would be on the man. But that last leap never came. The lion skidded in the soft sand. It stopped a mere step away. The lion raised its head. It looked at the man and licked his hand. It seemed like a miracle.

Who was the man? He was Androcles. And he remembered. Years before he had saved that lion. He lifted its right paw and saw the scar. Then he wrapped his arms around the lion's neck. Together, like partners, they walked around the whole arena. The crowds had never seen such a miracle. They cheered uncontrollably. It was the greatest show they had ever seen.

Main Idea   1

	Answer	Score
Mark the *main idea*	M	15
Mark the statement that is *too broad*	B	5
Mark the statement that is *too narrow*	N	5

a. Kindness will often be repaid, sometimes in unexpected ways. ☐ ____

b. Androcles' kindness was repaid when he faced the lion in the Colosseum. ☐ ____

c. Androcles was put into the Colosseum to fight the lion with a rock and sand. ☐ ____

Score 15 points for each correct answer.   **Score**

Subject Matter   **2**   This passage is mostly concerned with
        ☐ a. an event that took place in the Colosseum.
        ☐ b. the memories of lions.
        ☐ c. a description of the Colosseum.
        ☐ d. how spectators in the Colosseum acted.   _____

Supporting   **3**   In the Colosseum people watched
Details   ☐ a. men fighting.
        ☐ b. football games.
        ☐ c. lions fighting.
        ☐ d. wars.   _____

Conclusion   **4**   It is likely that the author of this passage admires
        ☐ a. stories about public shows.
        ☐ b. people who free the innocent.
        ☐ c. people who are kind to animals.
        ☐ d. large animals.   _____

Clarifying   **5**   The author describes what the Colosseum looks
Devices   like by using a
        ☐ a. list of adjectives.
        ☐ b. comparison.
        ☐ c. contrast.
        ☐ d. metaphor.   _____

Vocabulary   **6**   The lion's <u>bounds</u> are its
in Context   ☐ a. roars.
        ☐ b. legs.
        ☐ c. surroundings.
        ☐ d. leaps.   _____

Add your scores for questions 1–6. Enter the total here   **Total**
and on the graph on page 212.   **Score**   _____

32 Rubber and Charles Goodyear

Explorers found something strange in the New World. Indian children had balls that bounced. The explorers brought the material to England. Scientists worked with it. One gave it a name. He rubbed a piece of it over pencil marks. The marks rubbed off. He called the piece *rubber*. Rubber also kept out water. Scientists melted the raw rubber. They saw how to make raincoats. But there were drawbacks. The coats were sticky in hot weather. Cold made them stiff and <u>brittle</u>.

Could the problem be solved? Yes. Charles Goodyear solved it. He was a poor inventor. He worked in his wife's kitchen. She wanted him to find a paying job. But he kept on trying. One day he had an accident. He spilled a sulfur-rubber mixture on a hot stove. The sulfur smelled awful. His wife was angry. He was upset. Then he noticed something. The mixture baked like a pancake. He thought, "Why didn't it melt further?" He carefully lifted the pancake of rubber. It had changed. Now it was soft. It bent easily. He put it on ice. It did not stiffen. He held it over heat. It did not become sticky. The problem was solved. The rubber was "cured." It stayed tough and firm. Goodyear named the process after Vulcan. He was the Roman god of fire.

Goodyear licensed his process. But he was no businessman. He gained very little. Lawsuits ate up his money. Not much more is known. But there is a bright spot. Something must have worked. His second son graduated from Yale. He was a well-known historian. Another son also did well. He adapted the sewing machine. It now made shoes.

Yes, there was sulfur in the rubber. But there must have been brains in the genes.

Main Idea	1		
		Answer	Score
	Mark the *main idea*	M	15
	Mark the statement that is *too broad*	B	5
	Mark the statement that is *too narrow*	N	5

a. Inventors are not always successful businessmen. ☐ _____

b. Charles Goodyear discovered how to cure rubber, but not how to make money. ☐ _____

c. Goodyear's sons went on to be successful, unlike their dad. ☐ _____

Score 15 points for each correct answer.   **Score**

Subject Matter   **2**   The best alternative title for this passage would be
      ☐ a. A Lucky Accident.
      ☐ b. Hard Work Pays Off.
      ☐ c. Brains Are All it Takes.
      ☐ d. Rubber Poses Problems.   _____

Supporting   **3**   The sulfur-rubber mixture did not melt on
Details   the stove because
      ☐ a. it was quickly removed from the heat.
      ☐ b. the stove was not hot enough.
      ☐ c. the heat made it strong and solid.
      ☐ d. Goodyear had covered the stove with oil.   _____

Conclusion   **4**   The writer suggests that Goodyear
      ☐ a. was interested in Roman mythology.
      ☐ b. was the strong person in his marriage.
      ☐ c. was more successful at passing on his
          intelligence than being a businessman.
      ☐ d. enjoyed solving problems more than
          creating new inventions.   _____

Clarifying   **5**   The author uses the expression "like a pancake"
Devices   in order to show
      ☐ a. how fluffy the rubber mixture was.
      ☐ b. how flat and solid the rubber mixture was.
      ☐ c. how dirty the mixture looked.
      ☐ d. why Goodyear was heating the rubber
          mixture on a stove.   _____

Vocabulary   **6**   When something is <u>brittle</u> it is
in Context   ☐ a. like candy.
      ☐ b. easily breakable.
      ☐ c. mushy.
      ☐ d. warm.   _____

Add your scores for questions 1–6. Enter the total here   **Total**
and on the graph on page 212.   **Score**   _____

33 Collectible Cars

Many people like unusual cars. These are cars not made in large numbers. There are reasons only a few were made. Some of the cars were fancy and expensive. Others never caught on with the public. Many people collect such cars.

One fancy car was the Avanti. It was made by Studebaker. (This was a car company from the 1920s to the 1960s.) The Avanti was a sports coupe. It had sleek, curvy lines. It had a fiberglass body. The car was first sold in 1962. Then Studebaker closed. But the Avanti did not go away. A small factory kept making it. This factory was in Indiana. It made the cars by hand. It made about 50 cars a year. These cars were very expensive. But their owners loved them. The style did not change much from year to year. These cars quickly became classics. They are worth a lot of money today.

Another classic is the Edsel. This car came out in 1957. It was made by Ford. It was named after Henry Ford's son. Most car grilles go across the car's front. The Edsel's grille was <u>vertical</u>. Ford talked a lot about the car before it came out. They said it was "all new." But people did not like it. It did not look new to them. In fact, it looked ugly. It also did not run well. And it was expensive. The economy was not doing well. People wanted cheaper cars. They also wanted smaller cars. The Edsel did not last. It was only made for 3 years. But some people now like this car. It is rare. Only 110,000 were made. People collect it. There are Edsel clubs. What might this tell us? Maybe this. If something is old and rare enough, someone will want it.

Main Idea	1		Answer	Score
	Mark the *main idea*		M	15
	Mark the statement that is *too broad*		B	5
	Mark the statement that is *too narrow*		N	5

a. The Avanti and the Edsel are two popular collectible cars. ☐ _____

b. In contrast to the Avanti, the public did not like the Edsel. ☐ _____

c. Many old cars have value to collectors. ☐ _____

Score 15 points for each correct answer. Score

Subject Matter 2 This passage is mainly about
☐ a. how old cars were built.
☐ b. why the Edsel was a failure.
☐ c. a description and history of the Avanti and Edsel.
☐ d. handmade cars. _____

Supporting 3 The Avanti was made
Details
☐ a. by Ford.
☐ b. in a small factory in Indiana.
☐ c. with recycled Studebaker parts.
☐ d. with a strange-looking grille. _____

Conclusion 4 The author's feeling about the Edsel's current popularity is one of
☐ a. anger.
☐ b. surprise.
☐ c. bitterness.
☐ d. enthusiasm. _____

Clarifying 5 The basic pattern used to develop this passage is
Devices
☐ a. chronological order.
☐ b. a personal narrative.
☐ c. comparison and contrast.
☐ d. question and answer. _____

Vocabulary 6 The word <u>vertical</u> means
in Context
☐ a. up and down.
☐ b. from left to right.
☐ c. set at an angle.
☐ d. using wavy lines. _____

Add your scores for questions 1–6. Enter the total here and on the graph on page 212. Total Score _____

34 The Coffee Bean

How much coffee does an average American drink? That is, on a yearly basis. If you said, "about 15 pounds," you would be right. Now for a harder question. How many pounds does the United States use each year? The answer: almost 3 billion pounds.

The coffee plant is a shrub. The shrub is <u>pruned</u> to keep it under 12 feet. It was first found growing wild in Ethiopia. The seeds were brought back and planted in South America. Brazil is now by far the biggest producer.

We see the coffee bean. But we don't see the process that makes the clean bean possible. Here's what is needed. First, the berries must be picked by hand. Then they are put into water. The good sink to the bottom. Sticks, leaves, green, and bad berries float on top. The bean is inside a berry that looks like a cherry. This outer skin and pulp must be removed. Each cherrylike berry contains two beans. These beans have to be fermented and washed. The beans themselves have a thin skin. These inner skins must be removed too. Next, the beans are roasted. They're roasted at 900 degrees F. Finally, the beans are ready for sale. They may be sold whole. Or they may be ground for drip, fine, or regular coffee.

Coffee contains caffeine. It is a stimulant. The drink expands the blood vessels. More blood flows to the head and brain. Coffee keeps most people awake. This was first noticed in Ethiopia. Goats that ate the leaves and berries stayed awake all night.

Is coffee safe? Some studies say a cup or two a day is okay. But no one knows for sure.

Main Idea	1		
		Answer	Score
	Mark the *main idea*	M	15
	Mark the statement that is *too broad*	B	5
	Mark the statement that is *too narrow*	N	5
	a. Coffee beans come from a plant.	☐	_____
	b. Coffee comes from a process of cleaning and roasting beans.	☐	_____
	c. The coffee bean is inside a berry that looks like a cherry.	☐	_____

Subject Matter   **2**   This passage is mostly about
- ☐ a. how much coffee Americans drink.
- ☐ b. how coffee beans are cleaned and roasted.
- ☐ c. a study on whether coffee is safe or not.
- ☐ d. caffeine's effect on humans.

_____

Supporting Details   **3**   Just before the coffee bean is roasted, it
- ☐ a. is ground.
- ☐ b. has its inner skin removed.
- ☐ c. is fermented.
- ☐ d. is picked by a machine.

_____

Conclusion   **4**   We can conclude from this passage that
- ☐ a. all Americans drink 15 pounds of coffee a day.
- ☐ b. we drink too much coffee.
- ☐ c. there are no hard facts on whether coffee is good for you.
- ☐ d. Ethiopians drink more coffee than Americans.

_____

Clarifying Devices   **5**   This passage is mostly developed by
- ☐ a. telling the history of the coffee bean.
- ☐ b. a series of questions and answers.
- ☐ c. describing in detail the results of an ongoing study.
- ☐ d. explaining a process.

_____

Vocabulary in Context   **6**   In this passage <u>pruned</u> means
- ☐ a. ate the fruit of.
- ☐ b. removed branches.
- ☐ c. measured.
- ☐ d. warmed up.

_____

Add your scores for questions 1–6. Enter the total here and on the graph on page 212.   **Total Score** _____

35 Camels and Their Humps

Nature works in strange ways. Camels were given humps. Why? Humps provide a place to store food and water. Other animals store food and water differently. They use their tissues. These are all over their bodies. But camels have one special place. Their humps.

The Arabian camel lives mainly in the Sahara. It has one hump. There is a camel with two humps. It is the Bactrian. It lives in the Gobi Desert. That is in Asia. It is in Inner and Outer Mongolia. There is a camel's picture on a package of dates. That is a dromedary. It is a special camel. It is raised only for Army troops and racing. It can run 10 miles per hour. It can cover 100 miles in a day. In all these camels, the hump has one purpose. It stores food and water.

Camels can go for a week or more with no food or water. The hump doesn't carry plain water. But water is indeed stored there. Wait! What goes? Water or no water?

Here is the answer. The water is in the form of fat. On long marches, the camel makes water from it. How, you ask? Well, you've seen fat <u>splutter</u> in a frying pan. The spluttering is caused by water escaping from the fat. Something of this sort occurs inside the body of a camel. The fat breaks down. Water is released.

So the camel gets water from its hump. It also gets food from its hump. After a week or two, what happens? The hump gets smaller. After two weeks, the hump almost disappears. There is nothing left to form it. But by then it shouldn't matter. The long trip in the hot desert sands should be over.

Main Idea	1	Answer	Score
	Mark the *main idea*	M	15
	Mark the statement that is *too broad*	B	5
	Mark the statement that is *too narrow*	N	5
	a. There are several types of camels.	☐	___
	b. All camels have at least one hump.	☐	___
	c. The hump provides water and food for camels.	☐	___

Subject Matter   **2**   Another good title for this passage might be
- ☐ a. The Camel's Helpful Hump.
- ☐ b. Desert Days.
- ☐ c. How the Camel Got Its Hump.
- ☐ d. Cooling Down the Camel.   _____

Supporting Details   **3**   Camels with two humps
- ☐ a. have more water.
- ☐ b. are better for racing.
- ☐ c. live in Asia.
- ☐ d. can travel farther.   _____

Conclusion   **4**   You can assume that camels would
- ☐ a. provide good transportation in the desert.
- ☐ b. prefer living in a cooler place.
- ☐ c. need more water after each day of travel.
- ☐ d. not need to store food and water in colder places.   _____

Clarifying Devices   **5**   The author makes a comparison to fat in a frying pan in order to
- ☐ a. tell how heat affects the camel.
- ☐ b. suggest why the camel's body needs fat and water for long trips.
- ☐ c. demonstrate how the camel's hump provides it with water.
- ☐ d. explain the difference between water and fat.   _____

Vocabulary in Context   **6**   Splutter means to
- ☐ a. melt.
- ☐ b. heat up.
- ☐ c. bubble.
- ☐ d. cool off.   _____

Add your scores for questions 1–6. Enter the total here and on the graph on page 212.   **Total Score**   _____

36 Communicating with Horses

Ever hear of Monty Roberts? Probably not. Not many people have. Roberts is the man who "listens" to horses. "Listen," of course, does not mean verbal language. Yet he and horses "talk" to each other. How? Through the use of body language.

Here is why Roberts learned the sign language of horses. He hated the cruelty of "breaking" a horse. Breaking meant breaking a horse's spirit. To the old bronco busters, this was the only way. But it was a cruel way. A horse would be driven into a <u>corral</u>. It would be lassoed. Then it would be tied to a post. The buster would get on. He would wear a pair of spurs. Then the battle would begin. The horse would panic. It would try to throw the buster off its back. The horse when broken would never trust people again. An imprint had been made on its brain. People meant pain. Horses feared people.

Roberts, though, believed in a gentle way. He wanted to gain the horse's trust. He wanted to show that he would not hurt it. That a man could be a friend. Roberts's gentle way uses body language. Here is how he learned what to do. He watched a herd of wild mustangs. He went out into the high Nevada desert. He was only 14. He spent three weeks alone. He carried simple food with him. When he found the herd, he hobbled his packhorses. Then he crept forward. He got to within a quarter of a mile of the herd. He looked through his binoculars. The mustangs seemed very close by. He could see the smallest movements of their heads and ears.

Roberts watched the horses intently. He learned a great deal about their behavior.

Main Idea	1		
		Answer	**Score**
	Mark the *main idea*	M	15
	Mark the statement that is *too broad*	B	5
	Mark the statement that is *too narrow*	N	5

a. Monty Roberts "listened" to horses by watching them closely. ☐ _____

b. Monty Roberts searched for a gentler way of breaking horses. ☐ _____

c. Breaking horses is a difficult, challenging task. ☐ _____

Subject Matter   **2**   This passage is mainly about
- ☐ a. teaching horses.
- ☐ b. looking for a new way to communicate with horses.
- ☐ c. bronco busters of the past.
- ☐ d. sign language.   _____

Supporting Details   **3**   Monty Roberts first learned the language of horses by
- ☐ a. reading many books on the topic.
- ☐ b. taking pictures of wild mustangs.
- ☐ c. watching them from a distance.
- ☐ d. treating horses gently and in a friendly manner.   _____

Conclusion   **4**   From this passage, we can guess Monty Roberts
- ☐ a. was patient and gentle.
- ☐ b. knew a lot of bronco busters.
- ☐ c. was once afraid of horses.
- ☐ d. grew up in the East.   _____

Clarifying Devices   **5**   The author presents the old method of breaking horses by
- ☐ a. describing the process.
- ☐ b. explaining how quickly it went.
- ☐ c. telling a story about an old bronco buster.
- ☐ d. trying to persuade the reader of its advantages.   _____

Vocabulary in Context   **6**   A corral is a
- ☐ a. stable.
- ☐ b. large open space.
- ☐ c. barn.
- ☐ d. fenced-in field.   _____

Add your scores for questions 1–6. Enter the total here and on the graph on page 212.   **Total Score** _____

37 The Dun-Colored Mare

Monty Roberts watched a herd of mustang because he wanted to learn their habits. And soon a drama began to unfold. This incident gave Roberts the key to the language of the horse.

A light bay colt was behaving badly. He ran at a filly and gave her a kick. The poor filly just hobbled off. The colt seemed to puff up. He looked pleased with himself. He was looking for trouble. Then a little foal came toward him. The foal moved his mouth in a sucking action. This showed he was no threat. The sucking action meant, "I'm just a little foal." The bay colt had other ideas. He took a bite out of the foal's backside. The bay colt pretended nothing happened. With head down, he kept cropping grass. He looked <u>neutral</u>. He was trying to avoid blame. Roberts was fascinated. He was watching a big family drama.

Roberts shifted his sight to a big dun mare. He had noticed that she was the leader. When she moved, everyone followed. This mare was eating too. But she was slowly weaving closer to the colt. Monty felt sure the mare had seen everything. She showed no outward sign, but she kept edging closer to the colt all the time.

The dun mare was now only 20 yards away. But the colt tried another trick. This time he launched at a full-grown mare. He grabbed her by the nape of her neck and bit down hard.

The dun mare did not hesitate. She ran full speed at the colt and knocked him to the ground. The surprised colt struggled to his feet. The mare quickly whirled and charged again. Down went the colt again. Roberts's heart was beating fast. What a drama he was observing!

Main Idea	1		
		Answer	**Score**
	Mark the *main idea*	M	15
	Mark the statement that is *too broad*	B	5
	Mark the statement that is *too narrow*	N	5

a. The colt caused trouble in the herd by running at and biting a filly. ☐ _____

b. Roberts felt that watching the horses was like watching a drama. ☐ _____

c. Roberts watched a leader, a dun mare, punish an unruly bay colt. ☐ _____

Subject Matter **2** The best alternate title for this passage is
    ☐ a. Poor Little Filly.
    ☐ b. An Inside Look at a Horse Family.
    ☐ c. The Cowardly Colt.
    ☐ d. Mares in Charge.   _____

Supporting Details **3** The foal was "speaking" to the colt by
    ☐ a. flicking its ears.
    ☐ b. moving its mouth.
    ☐ c. cropping grass.
    ☐ d. biting and kicking.   _____

Conclusion **4** From this passage we can conclude that
    ☐ a. the other horses did not see the colt bite or kick the filly.
    ☐ b. the rest of the herd was not responsible for resolving the fight.
    ☐ c. the mare does not like colts.
    ☐ d. fights in the herd happened all the time.   _____

Clarifying Devices **5** The author compares the horses' actions to a drama because
    ☐ a. the mare is like an actress who is showing off.
    ☐ b. some horses are actors and some are the audience.
    ☐ c. it was a series of events involving conflict and emotion.
    ☐ d. Roberts was in the audience and the horses were pretending.   _____

Vocabulary in Context **6** In this passage <u>neutral</u> means
    ☐ a. dull.
    ☐ b. depressed.
    ☐ c. plain.
    ☐ d. uninvolved.   _____

Add your scores for questions 1–6. Enter the total here and on the graph on page 212.   **Total Score**   _____

38 The Wayward Colt

Monty Roberts watched the boss mare deal with an unruly colt. She drove the colt away, about 300 yards from the herd. She left him there alone and went back to the herd. She stood at the edge, leaving the colt in <u>exile</u>. The mare kept her eyes fixed on him. She faced him directly.

The colt's skin quivered. Being alone was like a death sentence. Wolves and mountain lions will get any horse that stands alone. The colt walked back and forth. Now, he held his nose close to the ground. Monty read this as a sign. It looked like a sign of, "I'm sorry. Let me come back."

The dun mare was unforgiving. The colt circled the herd. He tried to sneak back from the other side. But the mare was there too. She never once took her eyes off him. Roberts saw the colt doing a lot of tongue licking and chewing. Yet he had eaten nothing. Roberts wondered, "Is this a signal of humility?" He began to realize that every horse's movement had a meaning.

Roberts remembered when the colt was first driven out. The colt threw his nose out in a circular motion. Roberts read this as a sign of, "I really didn't mean it. It just happened." He remembered the position of the mare's body. It was in a straight line, meaning "stay away." Then he saw the mare's eye slide back along the colt's neck. This meant, "I'm letting you back." But first the colt had to put his nose to the ground again to say, "I'm truly sorry. Let me come back."

Roberts was excited. He saw the signs and the responses. He thought, "I'll use the same body and eye positions. Perhaps I too can 'talk to the horses.'"

Main Idea	1		
		Answer	Score
	Mark the *main idea*	M	15
	Mark the statement that is *too broad*	B	5
	Mark the statement that is *too narrow*	N	5

a. When the horse's nose moves around in a circle it is a way of communicating. ☐ _____

b. Roberts watched the horses and learned some of their "language." ☐ _____

c. The language of the horse involves many signs and signals that are all important. ☐ _____

Subject Matter   **2**   This passage deals mostly with
- ☐ a. learning to understand horses' body language.
- ☐ b. learning sign language.
- ☐ c. trying to talk to horses.
- ☐ d. why horses punish each other.   _____

Supporting Details   **3**   When the colt put its nose to the ground it was saying,
- ☐ a. "It just happened."
- ☐ b. "Come back."
- ☐ c. "I'm sorry."
- ☐ d. "Stay away."   _____

Conclusion   **4**   In the last paragraph the writer implies that Roberts
- ☐ a. had finished watching the colt and mare.
- ☐ b. would attempt to "talk" to horses.
- ☐ c. was confused and discouraged.
- ☐ d. had a full knowledge of horse language.   _____

Clarifying Devices   **5**   To help the reader understand Roberts's discoveries the writer uses
- ☐ a. examples from Roberts's observations.
- ☐ b. vivid descriptions of horses.
- ☐ c. opinions from other horse experts.
- ☐ d. scientific facts.   _____

Vocabulary in Context   **6**   To be in <u>exile</u> means to be
- ☐ a. in the center.
- ☐ b. near the exit.
- ☐ c. left alone.
- ☐ d. in trouble.   _____

Add your scores for questions 1–6. Enter the total here and on the graph on page 212.   **Total Score**   _____

39 The Great Trial

Monty Roberts wanted to test his knowledge of horses. He had just rounded up 150 mustangs and felt this was his chance. He asked Ray Hackworth to watch him "talk" to the horses.

Roberts moved to the middle of a small round corral. A colt was let in, and Roberts took a bold step toward it. The colt took flight, cantering around the corral as close to the wall as it could. Roberts fixed his eyes on the colt's, keeping direct eye contact. The colt kept trotting.

Since the signals were working, Roberts took the next step. He slid his eyes back to the colt's neck, and the colt slowed. Roberts let his eyes drop back farther, and the colt slowed a bit more. Roberts was <u>elated</u>; so far so good. He then moved his eyes back to the colt's eyes, and they locked. Quickly the colt's pace increased. Roberts was sure they were "talking."

Roberts now waited for the final sign. If the colt start licking and chewing, this would be the signal that it wanted to come to Roberts. The colt had already trotted around eight times. Roberts saw its tongue briefly. Its jaws showed chewing action. It kept one ear fixed on the man's position. Would it make the final move? Yes! The colt's nose dropped to an inch above the ground. Roberts's heart was racing. He moved his eyes 20 feet in front of the colt and turned his shoulders to a 45 degree angle. The colt stopped, but Roberts did not look. Would the colt come to him? There was one step, then another. It seemed forever. Then Roberts sensed the colt's nose inches from his shoulder. He slowly turned and stroked the colt between the eyes, and the colt followed him around the corral. Roberts was overwhelmed: he knew how to "talk" to horses.

Main Idea   1

	Answer	Score
Mark the *main idea*	M	15
Mark the statement that is *too broad*	B	5
Mark the statement that is *too narrow*	N	5

a. It is a great feat to understand and communicate with horses. ☐ _____

b. Roberts stepped toward the colt and it ran around the corral. ☐ _____

c. When using the horse's language, Monty could "talk" to and understand horses. ☐ _____

Subject Matter   **2**   The topic of this passage is
    ☐ a. two men watching a horse.
    ☐ b. listening to animals.
    ☐ c. moving with horses.
    ☐ d. a colt and a man communicating.　_____

Supporting   **3**   To "talk" to the colt, Monty
Details
    ☐ a. whispered in its ear.
    ☐ b. watched the colt carefully.
    ☐ c. acted as the mare had done.
    ☐ d. stood at the edge of the corral.　_____

Conclusion   **4**   Monty's success with the colt probably meant that
    ☐ a. he was able to communicate with other
        horses as well.
    ☐ b. Ray Hackworth tried to "talk" to the colt next.
    ☐ c. his study was complete.
    ☐ d. he learned to talk to other animals the
        same way.　_____

Clarifying   **5**   The phrase "Roberts's heart was racing" means that
Devices
    ☐ a. his heart was filling up with blood.
    ☐ b. he was very frightened.
    ☐ c. he felt like his whole body was racing around
        the corral.
    ☐ d. his heart was beating quickly with excitement.　_____

Vocabulary   **6**   In the passage <u>elated</u> means
in Context
    ☐ a. very happy.
    ☐ b. nervous.
    ☐ c. relaxed.
    ☐ d. disappointed.　_____

Add your scores for questions 1–6. Enter the total here
and on the graph on page 212.

Total
Score　_____

40 Peanuts and George Washington Carver

Peanuts are popular. There are many reasons. They are tasty. They are easy to shuck. And they don't mess up your hands. That's why they're so good at a baseball game.

Peanuts are popular all over the world. Over 20 million tons are grown per year. Here in the United States, we grow over one-and-a-half million tons. Georgia produces the most.

Have we always grown so many peanuts? The answer is no. They became popular here shortly after 1900. One man gets credit for this. He is George Washington Carver.

Why did Carver work with the peanut? For one reason, he wanted to save the soil. Cotton took too much of its strength. It took nutrients from the soil. Carver wanted to find a cotton substitute. The peanut crop was the answer. Peanuts made the soil richer. Their roots drew and fixed nitrogen into the soil.

But Carver still had a problem. Farmers had to make a living. Carver had to prove that peanuts could bring in as much cash as cotton. So he put his science skills to work. He worked day and night in his lab. The work paid off. He found over 300 products that could be made from peanuts. Out of peanuts he created such foods as cheese, milk, flour, and even coffee. He also made products such as ink, dyes, soap, and wood stains.

Carver and peanuts were saviors. Any farmer could grow peanuts. Small farmers could plant, grow, harvest, and sell them. Big farmers, too. This was a cash crop for all.

Carver's work with the peanut caused big changes in the agriculture of the South.

Main Idea	1		
		Answer	Score
Mark the *main idea*		M	15
Mark the statement that is *too broad*		B	5
Mark the statement that is *too narrow*		N	5

a. Peanuts became popular in the United States around 1900 and remain so today. ☐ _____

b. Some crops do good things for the soil. ☐ _____

c. By developing uses for peanuts, Carver changed farming in the South. ☐ _____

Subject Matter   **2**   This passage deals mostly with
- ☐ a. popular foods.
- ☐ b. farming in the South.
- ☐ c. how peanuts became a popular crop.
- ☐ d. steps in growing peanuts.   _____

Supporting   **3**   Carver wanted a substitute for cotton because
Details
- ☐ a. people were hungry.
- ☐ b. he wanted to bring in more cash.
- ☐ c. farmers could not easily sell cotton.
- ☐ d. cotton took too many nutrients from the soil.   _____

Conclusion   **4**   We can conclude that peanuts
- ☐ a. are more than just popular baseball game
       snacks.
- ☐ b. can be eaten with other vegetables.
- ☐ c. helped many people make money.
- ☐ d. only grow in the South.   _____

Clarifying   **5**   To explain why Carver promoted the peanut, the
Devices   author
- ☐ a. gives reasons.
- ☐ b. describes steps.
- ☐ c. explains the problems Carver faced.
- ☐ d. tells about Carver's life.   _____

Vocabulary   **6**   In the passage, the word <u>substitute</u> means
in Context   something that
- ☐ a. is almost the same.
- ☐ b. takes the place of something else.
- ☐ c. is better than something else.
- ☐ d. works with something else.   _____

Add your scores for questions 1–6. Enter the total here   **Total**
and on the graph on page 212.   **Score**   _____

41 Carver's Early Years

Who was George Washington Carver? Where did he come from? Let's start from the beginning. Carver was born of slave parents in 1859. Soon after his birth, night raiders stole the baby and his mother. The plantation owner, Moses Carver, was able to get the baby back. The mother could not be found. The plantation owners nursed the baby back to health. They treated him as if he were their own child. He was too frail to work in the fields, so he worked as the cook.

How did Carver become interested in education? As a child, he could not read, spell, or write. He was illiterate. But at the age of 10 he found an ancient speller. The plantation owners told him the words and their meanings. After that, he was on his own. He memorized each word.

It was now 1869. The slaves had been freed in 1865, so the boy was free to leave. He heard about a school in Missouri. It beckoned him. He bid a final good-bye. Then, barefooted, he tramped miles of dusty roads to the school. In town, as a cook, he earned food and shelter. He studied at night under a dim lantern. In only a year, he learned all that the school had to offer.

The next step was high school. But it was far away in Fort Scott, Kansas. Undaunted, he took to the road again. And again, as a cook, he found food and shelter. But school was not easy. He faced math and science and history. Everything was so new to him. Again, under the dim light of a barn lantern he studied. He worked and studied there for seven years. He was now 17. With diplomas under his arm, he returned home. He returned to the Moses Carver plantation. They welcomed him like a son. It was a restful summer. There he planned his next step.

Main Idea	1		
		Answer	Score
	Mark the *main idea*	M	15
	Mark the statement that is *too broad*	B	5
	Mark the statement that is *too narrow*	N	5

a.	Education was some slaves' way to freedom.	☐	_____
b.	George Washington Carver's parents were slaves.	☐	_____
c.	George Washington Carver worked hard to become educated.	☐	_____

Subject Matter   **2**   The best alternate title for this passage would be
- ☐ a. Education Is All You Need.
- ☐ b. Learning to Read.
- ☐ c. Learning in Spite of It All.
- ☐ d. A Breakthrough.

_____

Supporting Details   **3**   Carver became interested in reading when he
- ☐ a. was 12 years old.
- ☐ b. went to Fort Scott.
- ☐ c. went to school in Missouri.
- ☐ d. found an old speller.

_____

Conclusion   **4**   The passage suggests that during Carver's youth
- ☐ a. there were not many schools.
- ☐ b. many whites tried to educate blacks.
- ☐ c. all slave owners were mean.
- ☐ d. it was hard for a black person to get an education.

_____

Clarifying Devices   **5**   The meaning of the word "illiterate" is explained
- ☐ a. in the sentence that comes after the word.
- ☐ b. in the sentence that comes before the word.
- ☐ c. by telling a story about a speller.
- ☐ d. by examining its prefixes and suffixes.

_____

Vocabulary in Context   **6**   As used in the passage, the word <u>undaunted</u> means
- ☐ a. not understanding.
- ☐ b. frightened.
- ☐ c. not aware.
- ☐ d. bravely.

_____

Add your scores for questions 1–6. Enter the total here and on the graph on page 212.   **Total Score** _____

42 Carver's Legacy

George Washington Carver had a goal. This was to help southern farmers. They needed good crops. They needed crops that didn't hurt the soil. Carver went to Simpson College in Iowa. He studied there for three years. Then he went to Iowa State. He got two degrees there. The college knew he was smart. They wanted him to stay. He joined the staff. He was put in charge of a huge greenhouse. There he grew over 20,000 kinds of fungi. This work brought him much fame.

Carver had many job offers. Thomas Edison offered $175,000 a year. Henry Ford tried to hire him too. Stalin invited him to the Soviet Union. He wanted Carver to help with cotton. But Carver refused all offers. Instead, he took a job at Tuskegee Institute. This was a school for African Americans. Carver was paid only $1,000 a year. But he was happy. He had goals to reach. He knew he could reach them at Tuskegee.

Carver worked at Tuskegee for 47 years. He never asked for a raise in pay. And he never received one. He died on January 4, 1943. He died in his office chair.

Carver came up with over 300 products from peanuts. All could have been patented. He could have made millions. But he did not want to. Here is what he said. "Mr. Creator did not charge to grow the peanut. I cannot accept money for my work with it."

He wanted research to continue. He started a <u>foundation</u>. He gave his life's savings to it. This came to $40,000. One honor came after his death. His birthplace was made a national shrine. How surprised the humble Carver would have been!

Main Idea	1	Answer	Score
	Mark the *main idea*	M	15
	Mark the statement that is *too broad*	B	5
	Mark the statement that is *too narrow*	N	5

a. George Washington Carver devoted his whole life to achieving his goals. ☐ _____

b. Carver refused many job offers that would have made him rich. ☐ _____

c. Some scientists would rather do good than make a lot of money. ☐ _____

Score 15 points for each correct answer.   **Score**

Subject Matter   **2**   This selection is about
- ☐ a. Carver's life and research.
- ☐ b. growing peanuts.
- ☐ c. Tuskegee Institute.
- ☐ d. the many products that come from peanuts.   _____

Supporting Details   **3**   One job offer Carver accepted was working for
- ☐ a. Thomas Edison.
- ☐ b. Joseph Stalin.
- ☐ c. Tuskegee Institute.
- ☐ d. Henry Ford.   _____

Conclusion   **4**   From reading this passage you can guess that the author
- ☐ a. attended Tuskegee.
- ☐ b. admires Carver.
- ☐ c. is a researcher like Carver.
- ☐ d. knows a lot about peanuts.   _____

Clarifying Devices   **5**   The quotation from Carver suggests that he was
- ☐ a. a simple and humble man.
- ☐ b. a poor speaker of English.
- ☐ c. a narrow-minded person.
- ☐ d. a person used to a lot of attention.   _____

Vocabulary in Context   **6**   In this passage foundation means
- ☐ a. the base of a building.
- ☐ b. a kind of makeup.
- ☐ c. the money needed to start up a school.
- ☐ d. an organization that provides research money.   _____

Add your scores for questions 1–6. Enter the total here and on the graph on page 212.   **Total Score**   _____

43 The Mighty Amazon

The longest river in the world is the Nile. Its length is 4,160 miles. But the Nile is not the mightiest river. The Amazon is. The Amazon is also the second longest river in the world. It is 3,900 miles long. How long is that? It is longer than a road going from New York City to San Francisco.

The Amazon is mightiest for this reason. It flows the greatest amount of water. More water flows out to sea than from the Nile, Mississippi, and Yangtze rivers combined. That's a lot of fresh water! The force of its current is great too. The current can be seen 200 miles out in the sea. Here's a story to show the Amazon's amazing current. A sailing ship was far out of sight of Brazil. It ran out of drinking water. A passing ship drew alongside. The captain of the first ship asked for water. The captain of the second ship said, "Just dip your buckets over the side."

Here are a few more facts. At its mouth, the Amazon is 90 miles wide. Even up the river, you can't see the opposite bank. The river is also very deep—from 75 to 250 feet! During rainy season, the river rises about 53 feet more. Big ocean ships can sail about 1,800 miles upstream. Smaller ships can sail 1,000 miles farther.

What's the most bloodthirsty fish in the world? No. It's not the shark. It's the Amazon's piranha. It is only about four to eight inches long. It has razor-sharp teeth. And its jaws are <u>massive</u>. Thousands travel in a group. No animal can swim across the river. The fish will attack it. A 1,000-pound horse would be just bones in three minutes.

Are you planning a trip to the Amazon? Here's a good tip. Leave your bathing suit at home.

Main Idea	1		Answer	Score
	Mark the *main idea*		M	15
	Mark the statement that is *too broad*		B	5
	Mark the statement that is *too narrow*		N	5
	a. The Amazon is a mighty—and in many ways amazing—river.		☐	____
	b. In the world there are many well-known and famous rivers.		☐	____
	c. The Amazon has the greatest amount of fresh water in the world.		☐	____

Score 15 points for each correct answer.   **Score**

Subject Matter   **2**   This passage mostly deals with

☐ a. a comparison between the Amazon and the Mississippi.

☐ b. interesting facts about the Amazon.

☐ c. piranha in the Amazon.

☐ d. sailing in the Amazon.   _____

Supporting Details   **3**   The Amazon

☐ a. is surprisingly shallow.

☐ b. has many cities along its banks.

☐ c. is not as long as the Mississippi.

☐ d. is 90 miles wide at its mouth.   _____

Conclusion   **4**   After reading this passage it seems clear that

☐ a. people do not drink the Amazon's water.

☐ b. sailing on the Amazon requires a knowledge of its current.

☐ c. the Amazon flows through the rain forest.

☐ d. it would not be good to visit the Amazon during rainy season.   _____

Clarifying Devices   **5**   The writer helps you to visualize the length of the Amazon by

☐ a. telling how long the Mississippi is.

☐ b. describing its banks.

☐ c. comparing it to a distance on land.

☐ d. telling you how it compares to other rivers.   _____

Vocabulary in Context   **6**   In this passage <u>massive</u> means

☐ a. tiny.

☐ b. huge.

☐ c. useful.

☐ d. sharp.   _____

Add your scores for questions 1–6. Enter the total here and on the graph on page 212.   **Total Score**   _____

44 The Crusades

World War II was fought from 1939 to 1945. That is a total of seven years. We think that a seven-year war is long. But there have been much longer wars. For example, there were the wars called the Crusades. These wars went on for over 200 years. They started in the year 1097 and lasted until almost 1300.

You might wonder what the word *crusade* means. It comes from the Latin word *crux*, which means "cross." The cross was the sign of the Christians. Each soldier had a cross sewed on his jacket. This marked him as a Crusader.

The Crusaders were fighting the Turks. The Turks were Muslims. They had control of the Holy Land. The Christians wanted that land. They yearned to have control of the place where Jesus lived.

History shows that there were eight Crusades. Here is the reason. The First Crusade was a smashing success. Excitement ran high. Separate armies from England, France, and Germany set out. Some sailed. Some marched over 2,000 miles. (This is the distance from New York City to Salt Lake City.) The armies finally arrived at Jerusalem in 1099. They captured it after only six weeks. The Crusaders held the city for about 50 years. But many Crusaders sailed home. The remaining force was weak. The Turks fought to regain the city. They succeeded.

Seven more Crusades were <u>launched</u>. All failed. The Christians were never able to retake the lands they wanted.

Main Idea	1		
		Answer	**Score**
	Mark the *main idea*	M	15
	Mark the statement that is *too broad*	B	5
	Mark the statement that is *too narrow*	N	5

a. The First Crusade was the most successful of the eight that took place. ☐ _____

b. The Crusades were a series of wars. ☐ _____

c. The Crusaders' mostly unsuccessful fight for the Holy Land lasted over 200 years. ☐ _____

Score 15 points for each correct answer.   **Score**

Subject Matter   **2**   This selection is mostly concerned with
- ☐ a. the dangers of war.
- ☐ b. the Crusades.
- ☐ c. problems with lengthy wars.
- ☐ d. Christians who became Crusaders.   _____

Supporting Details   **3**   Crusaders were people who
- ☐ a. carried crosses into battle.
- ☐ b. were 12 years old or younger.
- ☐ c. fought for 50 years.
- ☐ d. wanted the land where Jesus lived.   _____

Conclusion   **4**   Judging from the passage, Crusaders
- ☐ a. were better at conquering areas than holding them afterward.
- ☐ b. are remembered mostly for the Fourth Crusade.
- ☐ c. joined the army because they were interested in traveling.
- ☐ d. enjoyed wearing the uniforms.   _____

Clarifying Devices   **5**   The author helps you understand how far the Crusaders marched by
- ☐ a. naming the countries they crossed.
- ☐ b. telling how long they marched.
- ☐ c. comparing it with a distance you are more familiar with.
- ☐ d. telling where they came from.   _____

Vocabulary in Context   **6**   In this passage <u>launched</u> means
- ☐ a. begun.
- ☐ b. put on boats.
- ☐ c. sent into space.
- ☐ d. considered.   _____

Add your scores for questions 1–6. Enter the total here and on the graph on page 212.   **Total Score**   _____

45 More Facts About Eskimos

Eskimos probably came to North America from Siberia. This does not mean they are Russian. There was once a land bridge there. The bridge connected Siberia and Alaska. The Eskimos simply crossed it. This was more than 10,000 years ago. Then the oceans rose. The Ice Age was over, and mountains of ice melted. The area is covered by water now, the Bering Strait.

The Eskimos settled near the sea. That was where the food was. They hunted seals. They even <u>hauled</u> in whales with harpoons. They also caught lots of fish. At times, hunting parties would go inland. One thing they hunted was caribou. The skins were prized for clothing. Why not use seal skins instead? Seal skins were very warm. But they were very heavy. Seal skins were best used for covering cold floors. Caribou skins were warm and much lighter. They were good to wear when traveling and hunting.

Caribou skins also made fine tents. These were used in the summer. In the winter, Eskimos lived in igloos. Igloos were made from blocks of hard-packed snow. The blocks were three feet long. They were one-and-a-half feet wide. They were about five inches thick. The blocks were fitted together. But they were not piled up straight. They were set in spiral form. The spiral became smaller toward the top. In this way, a dome was formed. You may wonder about light. How did it enter an igloo? The Eskimos used ice. They set a thin slab of it into a wall. This was the window. There was no danger of melting. The winter temperature is very low. It is about 20 to 30 degrees below zero. Eskimos live in one of the coldest and harshest regions in the world.

Main Idea	1	Answer	Score
	Mark the *main idea*	M	15
	Mark the statement that is *too broad*	B	5
	Mark the statement that is *too narrow*	N	5
a.	The Eskimos made their homes from blocks of snow in the winter.	☐	____
b.	Alaskan Eskimos learned how to adapt things in their environment to help them live.	☐	____
c.	Alaskan Eskimos lived in cold conditions.	☐	____

Subject Matter   **2**   In general, this passage is about
- ☐ a. igloos.
- ☐ b. how Eskimos hunted in winter.
- ☐ c. Eskimos' life in Alaska.
- ☐ d. the land bridge.   _____

Supporting   **3**   The igloo was made by
Details
- ☐ a. fitting snow blocks together.
- ☐ b. making thin slabs of ice.
- ☐ c. building the blocks straight up.
- ☐ d. forming blocks that were 5 feet long.   _____

Conclusion   **4**   What conclusion can you draw from this passage?
- ☐ a. Eskimos disliked living in Alaska.
- ☐ b. The winters were too hard for any other
       group of people.
- ☐ c. Alaska is not a place someone should visit.
- ☐ d. Eskimos were hardy and strong people.   _____

Clarifying   **5**   The author describes the Eskimos' homes by using
Devices
- ☐ a. steps in a process.
- ☐ b. comparison and contrast.
- ☐ c. a list.
- ☐ d. a firsthand story.   _____

Vocabulary   **6**   The word <u>hauled</u> means
in Context
- ☐ a. carried.
- ☐ b. caught.
- ☐ c. pulled.
- ☐ d. threw.   _____

Add your scores for questions 1–6. Enter the total here   **Total**
and on the graph on page 212.   **Score**   _____

46 The Inner Planets

There are nine planets in our solar system. But there are a lot of differences between them. Some people put the planets into two groups. They are called the inner and the outer planets.

There are four inner planets: Mercury, Venus, Earth, and Mars. All have rocky insides, or cores. Mercury is the smallest. It is also the closest to the sun. This planet has a great number of <u>craters</u> on its surface. The craters were caused by huge rocks. They crashed into the planet millions of years ago. Life is not possible on Mercury. The planet is 36 million miles away from the sun.

Venus is the next planet. It is about the same size as Earth. But it is very different from Earth. Venus is very hot, even hotter than Mercury. It is covered with thick clouds. These clouds are made of poison gases. Strong bolts of lightning constantly pass through the clouds. In the sky, Venus looks beautiful. It is often seen in the east just before sunrise.

Our own planet, Earth, comes next. It is 93 million miles from the sun. So far, it is the only place in our solar system where we are sure life exists. Almost three-quarters of its surface is water.

The fourth planet is Mars. It is about half the size of Earth, and much colder. It has two small moons. The surface of Mars is red. (Mars is sometimes called the Red Planet.) On the surface are many grooves. These look like beds of old rivers. Scientists wonder about these beds. Was there once water in them? Was there once life on Mars? They have sent probes to study Mars. One day we will know the answer to these questions.

Main Idea	1		Answer	Score
	Mark the *main idea*		M	15
	Mark the statement that is *too broad*		B	5
	Mark the statement that is *too narrow*		N	5
	a. Our solar system has nine planets.		☐	_____
	b. The four inner planets have both similarities and differences.		☐	_____
	c. The surface of Venus is much hotter than Earth's.		☐	_____

Subject Matter   **2**   This passage is mostly about
- ☐ a. the solar system.
- ☐ b. the outer planets.
- ☐ c. the inner planets.
- ☐ d. space exploration.   _____

Supporting Details   **3**   The surface of Mars has
- ☐ a. many craters.
- ☐ b. flowing rivers.
- ☐ c. many grooves.
- ☐ d. many places where lightning hit.   _____

Conclusion   **4**   Mercury cannot support life because
- ☐ a. of its pock-marked surface.
- ☐ b. it is too small.
- ☐ c. it has a rocky core.
- ☐ d. it is too close to the sun.   _____

Clarifying Devices   **5**   The author presents the planets
- ☐ a. in alphabetical order.
- ☐ b. in the order of their distance from the sun.
- ☐ c. in size order.
- ☐ d. by the shape of their orbit around the sun.   _____

Vocabulary in Context   **6**   <u>Craters</u> are
- ☐ a. deep holes.
- ☐ b. lakes.
- ☐ c. mountains.
- ☐ d. tiny planets.   _____

Add your scores for questions 1–6. Enter the total here and on the graph on page 212.   **Total Score**   _____

47 Oil and the *Elizabeth Watts*

The *Elizabeth Watts* was a cargo ship. And the word *cargo* meant that a ship carried dry goods. Dry goods were things like grain, steel, cloth, and shoes. These goods were always bundled and packaged. They could be stacked and secured. In stormy seas such a cargo would not shift. Shifting is a great danger at sea.

Not much is known about the *Elizabeth Watts*. But there is one thing she was noted for. She carried the world's first really big shipment of oil. She was not designed to carry oil, yet she did. She left the United States and arrived safely in England 45 days later. Some say she was lucky. There were no storms. The seas were calm.

She tried another oil shipment. She sailed. Beyond that the records are blank. It was noted that the captain had great trouble in getting a crew. Sailors <u>balked</u> at signing on with an oil ship.

To get a crew, the captain used an age-old method. He went from bar to bar. When he found a sailor, he plied him with free drinks of whiskey. Then he guided the staggering sailor up the gangway. By the time he woke, the ship was scudding on the high seas under full sail.

But what happened on the second voyage? No one knows for sure. Here is one explanation. The barrels of oil were tied in place by rope. During a storm, some ropes broke. The heavy barrels banged into each other. Some barrels burst, spilling oil. The metal barrels, crashing into each other, created sparks. Then the horror happened. The barrels caught fire and exploded. Nothing was left. Only the prayers of the sailors, flying upward like a flock of white doves.

Main Idea	1		
		Answer	Score
	Mark the *main idea*	M	15
	Mark the statement that is *too broad*	B	5
	Mark the statement that is *too narrow*	N	5

		Answer	Score
a.	The *Elizabeth Watts* carried oil and suffered tragedy because of it.	☐	_____
b.	Cargo ships have trouble carrying oil.	☐	_____
c.	The *Elizabeth Watts* was the first cargo ship to carry a large shipment of oil.	☐	_____

Subject Matter 2 This passage is mainly about
☐ a. the *Elizabeth Watts*.
☐ b. difficulties of ships carrying oil.
☐ c. travels over the Atlantic.
☐ d. problems with a captain and his crew. _____

Supporting Details 3 According to this selection
☐ a. captains had to trick crews to sail the high seas.
☐ b. the *Elizabeth Watts* carried the first good-sized cargo of oil.
☐ c. sailors today don't fear oil explosions.
☐ d. storms make cargo ships unsafe. _____

Conclusion 4 After reading the passage, the reader may conclude that
☐ a. early sailors preferred sailing on a ship carrying dry goods.
☐ b. the oil supply was limited because people would not work on ships.
☐ c. ship captains had to be mean in order to get a crew.
☐ d. the average trip to England by boat takes more than 45 days. _____

Clarifying Devices 5 The author develops the main idea in the passage by using
☐ a. many direct quotes.
☐ b. questions and answers.
☐ c. a story.
☐ d. arguments and proof. _____

Vocabulary in Context 6 The best meaning of the word balked is
☐ a. discussed at length.
☐ b. stopped short and refused.
☐ c. lined up for.
☐ d. were extremely disgusted. _____

Add your scores for questions 1–6. Enter the total here and on the graph on page 212.   **Total Score** _____

48 Black Pepper

Is the pepper plant a bush or a tree? This is a trick question. It is neither. It's a woody climber. It is not a vine. But it is close to it. It needs support. It reaches heights of 30 feet or more. The pepper plant is long lived. It bears berries for about 40 years. As a trade item, pepper has always been important. Overland caravans were used to get it. These caravans brought pepper from India to Europe. Pepper was so prized that it was used as money. Taxes were paid with it.

The pepper plant bears a small berry. It is about the size of a pea. When ripe, it turns red. The pepper berry must be hand-picked. Then it is dried in the sun. It turns black when it is dry.

Pepper plants need a long rainy season. The temperature needs to be high. The plants need shade, but not too much. They also need sun. Most of the pepper we use today comes from Java and Sumatra. We import about 30,000 tons each year.

Pepper was people's first means of refrigeration. During the Crusades pepper was used to preserve sausages. Meat packers use 25 percent of the pepper we import. It preserves the meat.

Pepper mills are now common items in the home. Restaurants used to use them too. But no more. The reason is this. Customers were "collecting" pepper mills. Now, a waiter comes around with a long pepper mill. He or she will sprinkle the pepper if wanted.

Pepper has also been used as a medicine. One old book recommends it. It says pepper will cure aches and pains. American Indians use it today to cure toothaches. It is also used by French and Dutch housewives. They use it to kill moths and to repel insects.

Main Idea	1		Answer	Score
	Mark the *main idea*		M	15
	Mark the statement that is *too broad*		B	5
	Mark the statement that is *too narrow*		N	5

a. The pepper plant's small berry turns black from the sun and heat. ☐ _____

b. Pepper is one of the most useful spices there is. ☐ _____

c. The pepper plant has been used for a long time and for various reasons. ☐ _____

Subject Matter **2** This passage is mainly concerned with
☐ a. pepper as a form of refrigeration.
☐ b. small inventions and improvements.
☐ c. pepper and its uses.
☐ d. pepper mills.

_____

Supporting Details **3** According to the passage, pepper has been used to
☐ a. pay taxes.
☐ b. make liquor.
☐ c. clean teeth.
☐ d. cure the stomach flu.

_____

Conclusion **4** Which of the following is implied but not stated in this passage?
☐ a. Pepper plants need sun and rain.
☐ b. The berries cannot be harvested by machines.
☐ c. Pepper preserves food.
☐ d. Pepper is not grown in the United States.

_____

Clarifying Devices **5** The author ends this passage by using
☐ a. a definition.
☐ b. an exaggeration.
☐ c. examples.
☐ d. comparisons.

_____

Vocabulary in Context **6** In the passage import means
☐ a. sell to a foreign country.
☐ b. bring from a foreign country.
☐ c. ship.
☐ d. buy.

_____

Add your scores for questions 1–6. Enter the total here and on the graph on page 212. **Total Score**

_____

49 The Groundhog

Everyone has heard of Groundhog Day. It is a minor American holiday. German and British settlers introduced it. Here is what they believed.

They thought that the groundhog awakens from its winter's sleep on February 2. The groundhog comes out of its hole. If the sun is shining, it will see its shadow. The shadow scares it. So it runs back into its hole. This means six more weeks of winter. If the day is cloudy, it will not see its shadow. Since it is not scared, it stays out of its hole. This means that spring will soon come. These are the same things we say on Groundhog Day today.

Groundhogs are strange animals. They are known mainly to country people. City people just don't know how to look for them. To the urban eye, a groundhog sitting stiffly by its hole may look like a root. It could also be seen as a clod of turf. Or it may look like a broken fence-post. But a farmer may see groundhogs anywhere he looks. They'll be watching like sentinels.

The groundhog is a native American. It is found in most states east of the Rockies. It may also appear as far north as Alaska. It is hated by farmers. The groundhog eats a third of its weight in a day. What an enormous appetite! It may eat about a half-ton of alfalfa in a summer. So 10 chucks in a big field would eat five tons.

Why do groundhogs eat so much? To prepare for winter. In the fall, when food is plentiful, they fill up. This extra food is changed to fat. This fat is what they live on during their long winter's sleep.

Main Idea 1

	Answer	Score
Mark the *main idea*	M	15
Mark the statement that is *too broad*	B	5
Mark the statement that is *too narrow*	N	5

a. There are many native American animals. ☐ _____

b. Besides appearing on Groundhog Day, the groundhog has some unusual traits. ☐ _____

c. Groundhogs eat a third of their weight in a day. ☐ _____

Subject Matter   **2**   This passage is mainly about
                          ☐ a. problems of the farmer.
                          ☐ b. American customs.
                          ☐ c. habits of the groundhog.
                          ☐ d. city people compared to country people.   _____

Supporting   **3**   To the city dweller, the groundhog is
Details   ☐ a. a big problem.
                          ☐ b. of great interest.
                          ☐ c. almost invisible.
                          ☐ d. a reason not to live in the country.   _____

Conclusion   **4**   It is obvious from the passage that farmers find
                          groundhogs
                          ☐ a. dangerous rodents.
                          ☐ b. undesirable because of their huge appetites.
                          ☐ c. useful to their fields.
                          ☐ d. clever and tricky animals.   _____

Clarifying   **5**   The author tries to stimulate the reader's interest by
Devices   ☐ a. telling the Groundhog Day story.
                          ☐ b. using a surprise ending.
                          ☐ c. using flowery language.
                          ☐ d. describing a process.   _____

Vocabulary   **6**   The word <u>urban</u> means
in Context   ☐ a. country.
                          ☐ b. farm.
                          ☐ c. city.
                          ☐ d. untrained.   _____

Add your scores for questions 1–6. Enter the total here   **Total**
and on the graph on page 212.   **Score**   _____

50 The African Elephant

What is the largest animal that lives on land? You most likely said, "The elephant." You are correct. (In the animal kingdom, only the whale is larger.) There are two kinds of elephants. First is the African elephant. The second is the Asian or Indian elephant. They are related. But they look different. The African elephant is bigger. Its ears are about four feet wide. Its tusks are about six to eight feet long. Our interest is with the African elephant.

An African male is about $11^1/_2$ feet at the shoulder. It weighs from 12,000 to 14,000 pounds. The largest ever measured stood 13 feet 2 inches tall.

The elephant has thick skin. It's about one inch thick. It's heavy. The skin alone weighs about a ton. Yet it is <u>tender</u>. The bite of a horsefly will draw blood. Elephants like to smear mud and clay over themselves. This protects their skin from bites by flies.

The elephant's trunk is about six feet long. It weighs about 300 pounds. The elephant uses the trunk in many ways. It smells, drinks, and feeds itself with its trunk.

The tusks (about six feet long) are really teeth. Only two thirds of each tusk stick out. The rest is in the skull. Tusks are used to dig for food. They are also used to fight. When trained, elephants can lift as much as a ton with their tusks. The molars (the grinding teeth) are about a foot long. Elephants have four molars. Each weighs eight to nine pounds.

The mother elephant gives birth after 20 to 22 months. At birth, the baby weighs about 200 pounds. It is already about three feet tall. It drinks its mother's milk until it is three or four years old.

Main Idea 1

	Answer	Score
Mark the *main idea*	M	15
Mark the statement that is *too broad*	B	5
Mark the statement that is *too narrow*	N	5

a. There are many large land animals. ☐ ____

b. Every part of the African elephant is large. ☐ ____

c. The skin of the elephant is thick but tender. ☐ ____

Subject Matter   **2**   This passage is concerned with
☐ a. elephants.
☐ b. large animals.
☐ c. Indian elephants.
☐ d. African elephants.   _____

Supporting
Details   **3**   The elephant's trunk is useful because it
☐ a. lifts heavy things.
☐ b. helps the elephant eat and drink.
☐ c. protects the elephant from flies.
☐ d. digs for food.   _____

Conclusion   **4**   You can **not** conclude from this story that
☐ a. baby elephants stay with their mother for
at least three years.
☐ b. a bee sting would not hurt an elephant's skin.
☐ c. elephants could use their tusks to lift a car.
☐ d. elephants do not like people.   _____

Clarifying
Devices   **5**   The author gives information about the African
elephant's trunk and tusks by
☐ a. explaining how they are used.
☐ b. comparing them to other body parts.
☐ c. comparing them to those of the Asian
elephant.
☐ d. telling a story about them.   _____

Vocabulary
in Context   **6**   If something is <u>tender</u> it is
☐ a. weak.
☐ b. thin.
☐ c. tough.
☐ d. sensitive.   _____

Add your scores for questions 1–6. Enter the total here   **Total**
and on the graph on page 212.   **Score**   _____

51 Elephants Alive and Dead

Wild elephants live in herds of 10 to about 50. The leader is usually a female. The herd can go through a forest quietly. It travels in single file. It goes about six miles an hour. When frightened, it may run at about 25 miles an hour. When they reach water, elephants swim across. They are great swimmers.

Elephants eat grass, leaves, small branches, and bark. They especially like the tender leaves on the top of trees. How do they get these leaves? They use their heads to knock trees down. They can easily knock down a 30-foot tree. Elephants also eat berries, mangoes, coconuts, corn, and sugar cane. They love salt. A wild bull eats from 500 to 600 pounds of food a day.

Many people want to find the graveyards of elephants. There is a strong belief that such graveyards exist. Here is why. Bones and tusks of dead elephants are almost never found. Searches have been made in forests. Grassy plains have been searched too. But neither bones nor tusks are found. Elephants don't live forever. Where are their bones? They don't just bury themselves. Here is one belief. Say an elephant gets sick or old (over 60 years). It <u>instinctively</u> knows death is near. It leaves the herd. It goes off to a secret graveyard. The place is known only to elephants, and perhaps other animals. But not to humans. Obviously, such a graveyard would be filled with ivory tusks. These were once very valuable. The objective of explorers was to find this "gold" mine. This graveyard belief may be a truth or a myth. But it is romantic. It would be nice if it were true.

Main Idea	1		
		Answer	**Score**
	Mark the *main idea*	M	15
	Mark the statement that is *too broad*	B	5
	Mark the statement that is *too narrow*	N	5
	a. The habits of elephants are interesting.	☐	____
	b. Elephants are interesting in both their lives and deaths.	☐	____
	c. Elephants live in herds and eat only vegetation.	☐	____

Subject Matter   **2**   Another title for this passage could be
- ☐ a. Where Do the Elephants Go?
- ☐ b. Vegetarians.
- ☐ c. The Best Swimmers.
- ☐ d. Bones and Tusks.

_____

Supporting Details   **3**   According to the passage, elephants like to eat
- ☐ a. rabbit.
- ☐ b. peanuts.
- ☐ c. corn.
- ☐ d. tree bark.

_____

Conclusion   **4**   The belief in elephant graveyards remains a mystery because
- ☐ a. people don't understand elephants.
- ☐ b. explorers have never found one.
- ☐ c. not many elephants die in the wild.
- ☐ d. it is more interesting not to know.

_____

Clarifying Devices   **5**   The author compares a graveyard to a "gold" mine because
- ☐ a. the graveyard is hidden like gold mines were.
- ☐ b. ivory tusks have been worth a lot of money.
- ☐ c. explorers like to dig in the ground.
- ☐ d. there may be gold hidden in the graveyard.

_____

Vocabulary in Context   **6**   Knowing something <u>instinctively</u> means to know it
- ☐ a. with help.
- ☐ b. very well.
- ☐ c. naturally.
- ☐ d. seriously.

_____

Add your scores for questions 1–6. Enter the total here and on the graph on page 213.   **Total Score** _____

52 Robert Fulton's *Clermont*

James Watt's steam engine (1769) <u>ushered</u> in a new age. The engine could do the work of hundreds of men and dozens of horses. So all was well on land. But not on sea. On sea, it was almost as in the time of Columbus. It was sailors pulling ropes, and the sails catching wind.

But in 1783, all this changed. A French nobleman created a steam-driven paddle wheel vessel. It was strong enough to buck a stiff river current. This nobleman pioneered the way. He wedded the steam engine to the paddle wheel. The news caught the imagination of Robert Fulton.

On August 17, 1807, the banks of the Hudson River were lined with people. They had read about Fulton's new boat. It was the *Clermont*. This ship had no sails. Instead it had two paddle wheels, one on each side. There were many doubters. There were many bets.

Smoke was already billowing from the stacks. Then, at the appointed hour, the ship's loud horn sounded. The nose of the 142-foot ship parted from the dock. The swift current of the Hudson caught the prow. The boat turned sideways. People held their breaths. Would the ship turn and be swept downstream? Fulton, an engineer, knew what to do. He gave full power to the water wheels. The handle of the tiller was full port. The ship's prow steadily fought the strong waters. Soon it pointed northward. Northward toward Albany. The crowd went wild.

The wheels were in rhythm now. The engine steamed. The ship went 150 miles up the Hudson from New York City. It took only 32 hours. Thus was born the first commercially successful steamboat. Robert Fulton had ushered in a new era in the history of transportation.

Main Idea	1		
		Answer	**Score**
	Mark the *main idea*	M	15
	Mark the statement that is *too broad*	B	5
	Mark the statement that is *too narrow*	N	5

a. The *Clermont* had paddle wheels propelled by a steam engine. ☐ _____

b. Transportation changed with the invention of steamships. ☐ _____

c. Robert Fulton's *Clermont* replaced sailing ships with steamships. ☐ _____

Score 15 points for each correct answer.

Subject Matter   **2**   The selection focuses on
- ☐ a. a ship ride to Albany.
- ☐ b. the steam engine.
- ☐ c. Robert Fulton's steamboat.
- ☐ d. paddle-wheel ships.

                                                   _____

Supporting Details   **3**   Robert Fulton launched his first successful steamboat in the year
- ☐ a. 1769.
- ☐ b. 1783.
- ☐ c. 1807.
- ☐ d. 1819.

                                                   _____

Conclusion   **4**   It could be concluded from this passage that steam power
- ☐ a. was Fulton's first invention.
- ☐ b. made transportation faster.
- ☐ c. was first used for water transportation.
- ☐ d. made Fulton rich.

                                                   _____

Clarifying Devices   **5**   The facts in this passage are presented in order of
- ☐ a. popularity.
- ☐ b. importance.
- ☐ c. interest.
- ☐ d. time.

                                                   _____

Vocabulary in Context   **6**   <u>Ushered</u> as used in this passage means
- ☐ a. led.
- ☐ b. married.
- ☐ c. followed.
- ☐ d. accompanied.

                                                   _____

Add your scores for questions 1–6. Enter the total here and on the graph on page 213.

Total Score   _____

53 The Water Woman

Does the name Mary Ludwig or Mary Hays mean anything to you? Probably not. Almost nobody knows her by these names. But the name Molly Pitcher should ring a mental bell.

Mary, or Molly, was born in New Jersey. She moved to Pennsylvania to work as a servant. There she married a young barber named John Hays. In 1775 the Revolutionary War started, and John enlisted. He spent the bitter winter of 1777–78 at Valley Forge. Like Molly, many wives joined their husbands there. They cooked, washed, and kept the camp clean.

Summer came. The army moved. It met the British at Monmouth, New Jersey. Records show that this day was the hottest in a century. The heat was fierce and the fighting was exhausting. The artillery smoke choked the soldiers. Their cries for water were pitiful. Molly heard and scooped up an old pitcher. She ran to a nearby spring and filled it. The water was gulped by parched throats. Cannonballs were tearing the ground. Musketballs were whizzing and thudding. Molly thought only of the hoarse cries, "Molly! The pitcher, please!" She kept running back with more water.

Molly glanced over and saw her husband fall. She saw no blood. She knew. Exhaustion and heat stroke were taking their toll. But he was breathing. She snatched the ramrod. She took his place. She cleared the barrel and shot volley after volley. The battle <u>lulled</u>. Mary went back to carrying water in her pitcher. John Hays now stood and leaned on Molly. Even he called her the name the soldiers had used. To him she would always be "my Molly Pitcher."

Main Idea	1		
		Answer	**Score**
Mark the *main idea*		M	15
Mark the statement that is *too broad*		B	5
Mark the statement that is *too narrow*		N	5

a. Molly carried the pitcher back and forth during the battle.	☐	_____
b. Molly Hays became Molly Pitcher after her bravery saved many lives.	☐	_____
c. A pitcher of water changed Molly Hays's name.	☐	_____

Score 15 points for each correct answer. **Score**

Subject Matter   2   This passage is mostly about
☐ a. the war.
☐ b. Molly Hays's names.
☐ c. how Mary's name changed.
☐ d. Molly's husband.   ＿＿＿

Supporting Details   3   Molly's husband was put out of action by
☐ a. a cannonball.
☐ b. the cold winter.
☐ c. a gunshot.
☐ d. heat exhaustion.   ＿＿＿

Conclusion   4   During the 1700s Molly's actions were even more honorable because
☐ a. women were not usually involved in battle.
☐ b. she was quite young.
☐ c. she was not bothered by the heat.
☐ d. men did not want women's help.   ＿＿＿

Clarifying Devices   5   This passage is developed by the author
☐ a. asking and answering questions.
☐ b. describing a scene of battle.
☐ c. telling events in chronological order.
☐ d. trying to explain women's role in the war.   ＿＿＿

Vocabulary in Context   6   <u>Lulled</u> in this passage means
☐ a. continued.
☐ b. quieted down.
☐ c. exploded.
☐ d. stopped.   ＿＿＿

Add your scores for questions 1–6. Enter the total here and on the graph on page 213.   **Total Score**   ＿＿＿

54 Ancient Trees

What is the oldest living thing on earth? If you said "the sequoia tree," you are very right. If you said "the redwood tree," you would be right too. But let's take it from the botanists. The redwood is in the Sequoia family. So sequoia is more correct. The tree is named to honor a Cherokee Indian who invented a system of writing.

There are two kinds of sequoia trees. First is the redwood. Second is the giant sequoia. The redwoods are the tallest. The giant sequoia is the biggest.

Redwoods grow to more than 300 feet. The trunks of many are more than 10 feet across. Giant sequoias are not so tall as redwoods. But their trunks are much larger. The world's largest tree overall is the General Sherman tree. It is about 275 feet tall. The trunk's diameter is 36.5 feet. But its seeds are only ¼ inch long. About 50,000 seeds weigh one pound. So big from so small!

The redwood and the giant sequoia live long. They have no known enemies. None has died from old age. Disease and insects have no effect. Though lightning has hit most tops, the trees just keep on growing. The General Sherman is about 3,500 years old. It dates back to 1500 B.C. The tree started to grow at the time of the pyramids of Egypt.

Numerous fires have swept through forests where redwoods and sequoias grow. Why weren't these trees burned like the rest? This is probably the answer. Their bark is from 6 to 12 inches thick. The fires have <u>charred</u> the bark over and over again. But the flames cannot reach deep enough to burn the live wood. What a coat of armor! Nature thought of everything.

Main Idea	1	Answer	Score
Mark the *main idea*		M	15
Mark the statement that is *too broad*		B	5
Mark the statement that is *too narrow*		N	5

a. The redwood and the giant sequoia are enormous, long-lived trees. ☐ _____

b. The giant sequoia is the largest tree in the world, larger than the redwood. ☐ _____

c. The sequoia trees have lived a long life. ☐ _____

Subject Matter **2** This passage is about
- ☐ a. old trees.
- ☐ b. the tallest tree.
- ☐ c. the redwood and the giant sequoia.
- ☐ d. the General Sherman sequoia.

_____

Supporting Details **3** The giant sequoia
- ☐ a. are taller than the redwoods.
- ☐ b. live the longest.
- ☐ c. are one of three kinds of sequoia trees.
- ☐ d. are the biggest trees overall.

_____

Conclusion **4** We can conclude that sequoia trees
- ☐ a. only grow in the best conditions.
- ☐ b. had a different name in 1500 B.C.
- ☐ c. can be killed by termites.
- ☐ d. can easily be cut down.

_____

Clarifying Devices **5** The author makes the point that sequoia tress can survive anything by presenting
- ☐ a. several different facts.
- ☐ b. detailed word pictures.
- ☐ c. scientific studies.
- ☐ d. old Indian stories.

_____

Vocabulary in Context **6** The word <u>charred</u> means
- ☐ a. killed.
- ☐ b. touched.
- ☐ c. burned.
- ☐ d. destroyed.

_____

Add your scores for questions 1–6. Enter the total here and on the graph on page 213. **Total Score** _____

55 The Wheel

We often hear, "So-and-so is a big wheel." We mean, of course, that the person is important. He or she makes things go around. Well, the real wheel also makes things go around.

Without the wheel, today's civilization would be impossible. Over 100 boxcars are loaded with cargo. One locomotive pulls them all. The 747 races down the runway. About 500 people are on a rocket with wheels and wings. How would these vehicles move at all without the wheel?

As children we'd jump on a bicycle or wagon and off we'd go. We never gave these wheeled vehicles a thought. Yet the wheel was a great invention! Who was the genius who thought of it?

There was no single genius. Things happened in bits and pieces. Some happened by chance and some by design. But it took hundreds and perhaps thousands of years of chance and insight.

Think of heavy dugout canoes and boats. They were rolled down to the shores on logs. There was no lifting or carrying. Just rolling. Some small chunks of log had rotted centers. Putting a sapling through two of these chunks made an axle. After that, it was easy. This was the beginning of the solid wheel. The time was the fourth millennium B.C.

The spoked wheel came next, in about 2000 B.C. The place was along the Tigris River in present day Iraq. Wheels with spokes were for chariots. These were the chariots for racing. These were the wheels for battle.

The solid wheel was first. After that <u>refinements</u> were a sure bet.

Main Idea	1		
		Answer	Score
	Mark the *main idea*	M	15
	Mark the statement that is *too broad*	B	5
	Mark the statement that is *too narrow*	N	5

a. The wheel is one of the great inventions. ☐ _____

b. The development of the wheel happened over time. ☐ _____

c. Spoked wheels were preceded by solid wheels. ☐ _____

Subject Matter   **2** Another good title for this passage would be
☐ a. What Is a Wheel?
☐ b. Bicycles, Wagons, and Chariots.
☐ c. The Real Wheel.
☐ d. How the Wheel Probably Developed.   _____

Supporting
Details   **3** The spoked wheel was
☐ a. developed in what is now Iran.
☐ b. invented by soldiers.
☐ c. faster than the solid wheel.
☐ d. first made from clay.   _____

Conclusion   **4** According to this passage the wheel
☐ a. tells us how people lived in the past.
☐ b. is a mystery to inventors today.
☐ c. is as useful as a lever.
☐ d. was improved upon little by little.   _____

Clarifying
Devices   **5** The author explains how the wheel developed by
☐ a. using notes from historic records.
☐ b. using imagination and ideas.
☐ c. describing what life was like before the wheel.
☐ d. explaining true stories.   _____

Vocabulary
in Context   **6** The best definition for the word <u>refinements</u> is
☐ a. discoveries.
☐ b. creations.
☐ c. developments.
☐ d. improvements.   _____

Add your scores for questions 1–6. Enter the total here   **Total**
and on the graph on page 213.   **Score**   _____

56 The Sea of Salt

What is the saltiest body of water in the world? Is it the Great Salt Lake in Utah? No. The answer is the Dead Sea. It lies between Israel and Jordan. It is six times saltier than the ocean.

What makes it so salty? Evaporation. The water, as vapor, rises. The solids, like salt, remain. Does any fresh water enter the Dead Sea? Yes. The Jordan River flows in from the north. Also, many springs bubble into it. These sources add about 7,000,000 tons of water daily. Wouldn't this fresh water make the Dead Sea less salty? No. Why? Because of the constant evaporation. As much water is evaporated as comes in. Also, the Jordan River and the springs bring in some added salt. They leach salt from the soil and rocks that they flow over.

The heat in the Dead Sea basin is extreme. Heat and the gases from the water give the sea a foul odor. Old reports say that no birds flew over the water. If they did, they would drop dead from the fumes. Fish are not able to live in the waters. They are too salty even for fish.

Despite its name and fumes, the Dead Sea is pretty. Its waters are smooth and sparkling. Some people believe the water can cure certain diseases. The hot springs are used for health reasons. A health resort is on the shore. Efforts are being made to expand the tourist trade. The winter climate is warm and dry. The scenery is awe-inspiring. The area is interesting. There is a cave on the West Bank. Here the famous Dead Sea Scrolls were found. The Dead Sea is mentioned in Biblical stories. Some of the Crusaders used the Jordan River and the Dead Sea in their travels. History is everywhere.

Main Idea	1		
		Answer	**Score**
	Mark the *main idea*	M	15
	Mark the statement that is *too broad*	B	5
	Mark the statement that is *too narrow*	N	5

a. The Dead Sea is the saltiest body of water in the world. ☐ _____

b. Some fresh water flows into the Dead Sea. ☐ _____

c. The Dead Sea is very salty. ☐ _____

Subject Matter   **2**   This passage is mostly about
- ☐ a. salty bodies of water.
- ☐ b. the Dead Sea.
- ☐ c. the Dead Sea Scrolls.
- ☐ d. the Jordan River.   _____

Supporting Details   **3**   The Dead Sea is salty because of
- ☐ a. bubbling springs.
- ☐ b. sulfur.
- ☐ c. fresh water.
- ☐ d. evaporation.   _____

Conclusion   **4**   This passage does **not** imply that people visit the Dead Sea because
- ☐ a. of its history.
- ☐ b. it can be healing.
- ☐ c. of its wildlife.
- ☐ d. it is beautiful.   _____

Clarifying Devices   **5**   The first few sentences of the second paragraph explain the meaning of
- ☐ a. "salty."
- ☐ b. "evaporation."
- ☐ c. "springs."
- ☐ d. "leach."   _____

Vocabulary in Context   **6**   The word <u>constant</u>, as used in the passage, means
- ☐ a. slow.
- ☐ b. careful.
- ☐ c. quick.
- ☐ d. endless.   _____

Add your scores for questions 1–6. Enter the total here and on the graph on page 213.   **Total Score**   _____

57 Perfecting the Steam Engine

You have heard of inventor James Watt. He built a successful steam engine in 1769. But the first baby step to this invention took place in Egypt. The year was 120 B.C. A man attached two pipes to an ordinary kettle. He hung a globe over it. The steam made the globe go around. The device served no useful purpose. It was just something to see. No one at that time saw the <u>potential</u>.

Over 1,800 years later, in 1698, Englishman Thomas Savery put steam to work. He patented the first steam engine. The engine pumped water from a coal mine. Soon others tried their hand at the work. In 1712, Thomas Newcomen, an English blacksmith, improved Savery's engine. The engine he built also pumped water.

James Watt, a Scotsman, then took a giant step. He improved the steam engine greatly. Let's see what he did. He started from scratch. At 18, he learned the trade of an instrument maker. At 21, he got a job at the University of Glasgow. Funny how mere chance plays such an important part in life. At least, it did for James Watt. Here is what happened in 1769.

Watt was lucky. A Newcomen steam engine was brought in for repair. Watt took it apart. He saw how it worked and repaired it. He knew he could improve it. There were technical problems. He asked students and professors for help. The result was an almost perfect engine.

Watt applied for a patent and got it. Then he teamed up with Matthew Boulton, who had experience in manufacturing. Together they formed a company. They rented out the design. The firm was highly successful. James Watt retired in 1800, a very wealthy man.

Main Idea	1	Answer	Score
	Mark the *main idea*	M	15
	Mark the statement that is *too broad*	B	5
	Mark the statement that is *too narrow*	N	5

a. James Watt became successful by greatly improving the steam engine. ☐ ____

b. James Watt was an instrument maker at the University of Glasgow. ☐ ____

c. When people take chances, new inventions and discoveries can be made. ☐ ____

Score 15 points for each correct answer.   **Score**

Subject Matter | **2** | Another good title for this passage would be
- [ ] a. The Cleverness of James Watt.
- [ ] b. Steps to a Perfect Steam Engine.
- [ ] c. Inventions That Work.
- [ ] d. Trying Something New.

_____

Supporting Details | **3** | Steam power was important because it
- [ ] a. led to the invention of the steam engine.
- [ ] b. made a globe go round.
- [ ] c. helped in automobile design.
- [ ] d. made others want to become inventors.

_____

Conclusion | **4** | It is apparent that James Watt
- [ ] a. didn't believe in trying new things.
- [ ] b. did not know how to take advantage of a situation.
- [ ] c. was both well-trained and clever.
- [ ] d. was not smart enough to invent anything on his own.

_____

Clarifying Devices | **5** | The facts in this passage are presented in
- [ ] a. alphabetical order.
- [ ] b. chronological order.
- [ ] c. spatial order.
- [ ] d. from the most to the least important.

_____

Vocabulary in Context | **6** | The word <u>potential</u> means
- [ ] a. future possibility.
- [ ] b. usefulness.
- [ ] c. immediate purpose.
- [ ] d. discovery.

_____

Add your scores for questions 1–6. Enter the total here and on the graph on page 213.   **Total Score**   _____

58 The Rare and Beautiful Diamond

Here is an old sales pitch: What is a girl's best friend? The answer: a diamond. Why is the diamond so popular? Because nothing sparkles like this gem. The reason it sparkles so brilliantly is because it reflects the light. It also bends the rays of light so they hit more surfaces and reflect from them. And finally, it breaks up the light into all the colors of the rainbow. Here is another <u>vital</u> fact: the sparkle must be created. To create it, skilled men cut as many as 58 sides or facets onto a diamond. There are 33 facets above the middle. The other 25 facets are below. All are highly polished.

There are some world famous diamonds. The world's largest stone is the Cullinan. It was found in 1905 in South Africa. It weighed 3,106 carats. This is equal to about $1\frac{1}{3}$ pounds. The stone was given to King Edward VII of England.

The gem that has the most exciting history is the Orloff. This stone was stolen by a French soldier. He first broke into a Hindu temple. Then he climbed onto a tall idol. With a wooden bar he pried out the idol's eye, which was the diamond. Somehow he got the gem back to France. He sold it to a dealer. The dealer sold it to Orloff, a Russian prince. Orloff paid over a half million dollars for it. He gave it to Catherine the Great, Empress of Russia, with whom he was in love.

The exact weight of the Orloff is 199.6 carats. It is seven eighths of an inch high. It is $1\frac{1}{4}$ inches wide. It is $1\frac{3}{8}$ inches long. The stone became the jewel of the Russian czars, the Romanoffs. It is now in a Russian museum. It is mounted in the royal scepter.

Main Idea 1

	Answer	Score
Mark the *main idea*	M	15
Mark the statement that is *too broad*	B	5
Mark the statement that is *too narrow*	N	5

a. Diamonds are very popular. ☐ _____

b. All diamonds sparkle, but the most famous are also large. ☐ _____

c. The Orloff diamond has an interesting history. ☐ _____

Subject Matter   **2** This passage is mostly about
    ☐ a. the Orloff diamond.
    ☐ b. how diamonds reflect light.
    ☐ c. diamonds and what makes them valuable.
    ☐ d. the world's largest diamond.   _____

Supporting   **3** Diamonds are popular because they
Details   ☐ a. are cut into facets.
    ☐ b. have the most interesting history.
    ☐ c. are the best known gem.
    ☐ d. sparkle.   _____

Conclusion   **4** This passage suggests that certain diamonds
became famous because
    ☐ a. of their weight.
    ☐ b. they were stolen.
    ☐ c. they were once owned by royalty.
    ☐ d. of their color.   _____

Clarifying   **5** To introduce the Orloff diamond the author uses
Devices   ☐ a. several examples.
    ☐ b. an interesting story.
    ☐ c. its dimensions and weight.
    ☐ d. information about where it was mined.   _____

Vocabulary   **6** If something is <u>vital</u> it is
in Context   ☐ a. expensive.
    ☐ b. constantly criticized.
    ☐ c. very important.
    ☐ d. factual.   _____

Add your scores for questions 1–6. Enter the total here   **Total**
and on the graph on page 213.   **Score**   _____

59 The World's Hardest Substance

The diamond is the hardest natural substance in the world. What causes this super-hardness? Pressure and heat are the answers. The pressure has to be close to two million pounds. That's per square inch. Much heat is required too. Experts say over 5,000 degrees. To make a diamond, one more thing is needed. This is black carbon. Pressure, heat, and carbon combine. They create a sparkling diamond. The very best are colorless. Pale blue stones—very rare—are high quality too.

Where do most diamonds come from? Over 97 percent come from Africa. The first diamond in Africa was not found by miners. Children found it, in 1866. They were playing in a <u>shallow</u> stream. One picked up "a pretty pebble." The "pebble" was placed on the mantel of the fireplace. It was soon forgotten. Much later, a guest noticed the sparkle. He urged the farmer to have the stone looked at. He did. He took it to an expert in town. The "pebble" proved to be a diamond worth $2,500. That was a small fortune in those days. To date, the mines in Africa have produced over 1 billion dollars worth of diamonds.

Not all diamonds are found in Africa. Our hemisphere produced diamonds too. Brazil was a big producer in earlier times. The famous gem the Star of the South was found in Brazil in 1853.

The gem The President Vargas was found more recently in Brazil. This was in 1938. A poor prospector found the stone. It was in the San Antonio River. It weighed 726.6 carats. The man sold the stone for $10,000 to a local broker. The broker almost immediately resold it. He got about $425,000. What a nice guy!

Main Idea   1

	Answer	Score
Mark the *main idea*	M	15
Mark the statement that is *too broad*	B	5
Mark the statement that is *too narrow*	N	5

a. Diamonds are valuable, hard, and are found in a few different countries. ☐ _____

b. The hardest natural substance is the diamond. ☐ _____

c. Diamonds have been mistaken for stones or pebbles. ☐ _____

Subject Matter **2** This passage is mostly about
- ☐ a. how to find diamonds.
- ☐ b. the hardest natural substances.
- ☐ c. stones from Africa.
- ☐ d. where diamonds have been found.   _____

Supporting Details **3** Diamonds are hard because of
- ☐ a. their lack of color.
- ☐ b. heat and pressure.
- ☐ c. black carbon.
- ☐ d. being in the ground.   _____

Conclusion **4** From this passage, we can assume diamonds
- ☐ a. can be found just about anywhere.
- ☐ b. are often found in rivers or streams.
- ☐ c. are all at least $2,000.
- ☐ d. are always white.   _____

Clarifying Devices **5** The writer explains where diamonds are found by using
- ☐ a. direct quotations.
- ☐ b. true stories.
- ☐ c. arguments.
- ☐ d. humor.   _____

Vocabulary in Context **6** In this passage the word <u>shallow</u> means
- ☐ a. very empty.
- ☐ b. unfriendly.
- ☐ c. not very deep.
- ☐ d. fast moving.   _____

Add your scores for questions 1–6. Enter the total here and on the graph on page 213.   **Total Score**   _____

119

60 Louis Braille, Alphabet Maker

Blind people can read. They do so by running their fingers along a line of raised points or dots on paper. Of course, they first have to learn the code. Here are some examples of it. One dot stands for the letter "A." Two dots side by side mean "C." Four dots arranged to look like a box (: :) stand for the letter "G." By placing the dots in special patterns, all the letters of the alphabet can be formed.

This code was made up by Frenchman Louis Braille. Though he could see at birth, he became sightless when he was only three. Braille was cutting leather in his father's shop. His knife slipped and cut his eye. Infection spread to both eyes, and he became blind.

At 10, he was placed in a home for the blind. But young Louis had great talent. He became a skilled musician and soon got a job as a church organist in Paris.

Because he had talent and was quick, he became a teacher at a school for the blind. While there, he heard that an army captain had sent messages to his gun crews so they could read them at night without light. His messages were in the simple form of raised dots and dashes. This was the clue Louis needed. At the age of 15, he worked out his own six-dot code. Each group of dots is called a cell. The cells are three dots high and two dots wide. For the rest of his life, Braille taught his young flock to read both written and musical works using his code.

For the last 17 years of his life, Braille was ill with tuberculosis. He died at the age of 43. France honored him by placing his remains in the famous Pantheon in Paris.

Main Idea	1		Answer	Score
	Mark the _main idea_		M	15
	Mark the statement that is _too broad_		B	5
	Mark the statement that is _too narrow_		N	5

a. Louis Braille developed a reading method for blind people. ☐ _____

b. Louis Braille became blind as a child. ☐ _____

c. Blind people can read. ☐ _____

Score 15 points for each correct answer. Score

Subject Matter **2** This passage is mainly about
- ☐ a. blind people.
- ☐ b. reading codes.
- ☐ c. Louis Braille and his alphabet.
- ☐ d. how blind people read. _____

Supporting Details **3** Louis Braille developed an alphabet for blind people after he
- ☐ a. became blind as a young child.
- ☐ b. worked as an organist.
- ☐ c. learned that soldiers could read messages from raised dots.
- ☐ d. became a skilled musician. _____

Conclusion **4** From this passage, you can conclude that
- ☐ a. all blind people read Braille.
- ☐ b. sign language is more useful than Braille to the blind.
- ☐ c. most students know that Louis Braille developed the Braille alphabet.
- ☐ d. Louis Braille wouldn't have developed the alphabet if he had not been blind. _____

Clarifying Devices **5** The author makes his point through
- ☐ a. comparison and contrast.
- ☐ b. negative arguments.
- ☐ c. autobiographical observation.
- ☐ d. a biography. _____

Vocabulary in Context **6** The best meaning of <u>flock</u> in this passage is
- ☐ a. a group of sheep.
- ☐ b. a number of blind students.
- ☐ c. many teachers.
- ☐ d. several blind musicians. _____

Add your scores for questions 1–6. Enter the total here and on the graph on page 213. Total Score _____

61 The Seven Cs of a Good Letter

What is the secret of writing a good letter? Here are two main ones. Don't try to be fancy. Don't try to impress your reader. You'll be successful if you follow these seven Cs.

Clear. Use short, direct sentences. Make them easy to understand. Talk as if the reader were right there with you. Above all, don't use an introduction.

Correct. Make sure what you say is correct. Don't guess, even for spelling. Flip open your dictionary. If you need to, check a reference book too. Use them as much as you need to.

Complete. Don't scatter your points. Finish one point completely before going on to the next. This is good organization too.

Courteous. Be friendly rather than <u>flippant</u>. Present your information nicely even if you are complaining about something. In all letters, treat others as you want them to treat you.

Concise. Make each point as clearly and briefly as you can.

Conversational. This is really the secret of good writing. Just "talk" to the person. Such a letter has a natural, friendly tone. Let your personality come through naturally.

Considerate. Think of the reader's point of view as you write. Write about what you believe the reader needs or wants to know. Try to be helpful. This will build good feeling toward you.

The seven Cs are about writing letters. But how about school papers? Use the seven Cs. Write as if you are talking to your teacher or professor. You'll be surprised. You'll almost instantly become a good writer. And you might even enjoy writing from now on.

Main Idea	1	Answer	Score
	Mark the *main idea*	M	15
	Mark the statement that is *too broad*	B	5
	Mark the statement that is *too narrow*	N	5

a. Writing a good letter involves seven steps. ☐ _____

b. The seven Cs will help one write a good letter. ☐ _____

c. The main secret to writing is to be yourself. ☐ _____

Score 15 points for each correct answer.   **Score**

Subject Matter   **2**   This selection is all about
    ☐ a. doing well in school.
    ☐ b. using the seven Cs.
    ☐ c. being yourself.
    ☐ d. enjoying writing.   _____

Supporting   **3**   According to this passage one secret to good
Details   writing is to
    ☐ a. try to sound impressive.
    ☐ b. "talk" to the person.
    ☐ c. include long sentences.
    ☐ d. have a strong introduction.   _____

Conclusion   **4**   Based on this passage we can assume
    ☐ a. letter writing is more important than other
        types of writing.
    ☐ b. writing should not be taken too seriously.
    ☐ c. the seven Cs are all you need to know to be
        a great writer.
    ☐ d. good letter writers can write papers well too.   _____

Clarifying   **5**   In this passage the writer presents information in
Devices   ☐ a. chronological order.
    ☐ b. a list.
    ☐ c. a series of comparisons.
    ☐ d. a description.   _____

Vocabulary   **6**   <u>Flippant</u> means
in Context   ☐ a. serious.
    ☐ b. crude.
    ☐ c. speedy.
    ☐ d. overly casual.   _____

Add your scores for questions 1–6. Enter the total here   **Total**
and on the graph on page 213.   **Score**   _____

62 Stories of the Moon

Did you ever hear this old saying? "The moon is made of green cheese." People used to say this until about 1969. Then the first explorers landed on the moon. We learned different things about the moon's surface then. For instance, we found it was hard and rough. It has many craters.

The moon is Earth's only natural satellite. Its diameter is roughly one-fourth that of Earth. Its <u>gravity</u> is much less. Astronauts on the moon's surface bounced rather than walked.

The moon circles Earth on the average of once every 29 days. Its orbit around Earth is not circular; it is more of an oval. So the moon's distance from Earth can vary quite a bit. Sometimes it is about 250,000 miles from Earth. Other times it is only 220,000 miles away.

The back side of the moon always faces away from Earth. But this does not mean it is always dark. The moon gets its light from the sun, just like everything else in our solar system.

Eclipses of the moon are fairly common. These happen when Earth comes between the sun and the moon. Then some or all of the moon's light is blocked.

Usually we see one full moon a month. Certain types of full moons have specific names. The Harvest Moon, for instance, is the moon nearest the fall equinox (about September 22). For several days after it, the moon rises soon after sunset. This provides extra hours of light to farmers harvesting their crops. The Hunter's Moon is the next full moon after that. The light then is pretty similar to Harvest Moon light. A Blue Moon is not really blue. It is the name given to the second full moon in a month. Sometimes two or three years pass before we get a Blue Moon.

Main Idea	1	Answer	Score
	Mark the _main idea_	M	15
	Mark the statement that is _too broad_	B	5
	Mark the statement that is _too narrow_	N	5

a. There are many interesting facts about our moon. ☐ _____

b. The moon is not made of green cheese. ☐ _____

c. Some planets in our solar system have moons. ☐ _____

Subject Matter   **2**   This passage deals mostly with
☐ a. moon exploration.
☐ b. facts about the moon.
☐ c. different kinds of full moons.
☐ d. gravity on the moon.
_____

Supporting Details   **3**   A Blue Moon
☐ a. has a faint bluish color.
☐ b. rises soon after sunset.
☐ c. always follows a Hunter's Moon.
☐ d. does not occur regularly.
_____

Conclusion   **4**   Earth comes between the sun and the moon
☐ a. almost never.
☐ b. only when there is a full moon.
☐ c. somewhat often.
☐ d. nearly always in the winter.
_____

Clarifying Devices   **5**   The information in the first paragraph is developed through a
☐ a. comparison.
☐ b. short, untrue story.
☐ c. list of facts.
☐ d. vivid description.
_____

Vocabulary in Context   **6**   The word <u>gravity</u> has to do with
☐ a. an amount of light.
☐ b. a force that holds things down.
☐ c. a smooth surface.
☐ d. a rate of speed.
_____

Add your scores for questions 1–6. Enter the total here and on the graph on page 213.   **Total Score**   _____

63 The Miller's Problem

Records show that the windmill was first used in Persia in A.D. 644. From there it was taken back to China by Genghis Khan. In China it was used to lift water to irrigate the land. In Holland it was used for the opposite purpose. It drained the water off the land.

Lifting water onto or off the land takes a lot of power. And the windmill was the answer. The windmill uses the energy of the wind to produce power for humans to use.

The windmills in Holland were built with four long arms. With canvas "sails" on the arms, the wind was captured to turn the millstone. Canvas was a good material. It was strong yet light. But it was not the final answer. The canvas sail had a drawback. Sometimes the winds reached gale force. Unless the canvas sails were rolled up, the entire windmill could be tossed on its side.

Sea captains faced the same danger. Unless they trimmed their sails, the masts would squirm out of their sockets and tumble overboard. The captain could adjust his sails to shorten the canvas, but the miller's task was not that simple. First, he had to shut down his mill. He did so by braking the wind shaft. The brakes were two wooden blocks called cheeks. If they were applied too quickly, the sails would come to a quick stop. The wind would then tear them to shreds.

The danger was removed by using wooden blinds in the place of canvas. As modern window blinds control the passage of light, so the wooden mill blinds controlled the passage of air. If a storm arose, the blinds were opened and the blast passed harmlessly through the sails. If the winds were calm, the blinds were closed to capture every breath.

Main Idea 1

	Answer	Score
Mark the *main idea*	M	15
Mark the statement that is *too broad*	B	5
Mark the statement that is *too narrow*	N	5

a. Windmills have been used for many years. ☐ _____

b. The windmill was used to turn the millstone. ☐ _____

c. The windmill became more useful when wooden blinds replaced canvas sails. ☐ _____

Subject Matter 2 The main focus of this passage is
☐ a. designing windmills to prevent damage.
☐ b. turning the millstone with wind.
☐ c. a history of windmills.
☐ d. comparing Chinese and Dutch windmills. _____

Supporting Details 3 The brakes used to slow down the windmill shaft were called
☐ a. discs
☐ b. shoes.
☐ c. axles.
☐ d. cheeks. _____

Conclusion 4 A windmill is similar to a sailing ship because
☐ a. both are wind powered.
☐ b. the sails of both are identical.
☐ c. both use wooden brakes.
☐ d. both use blinds to control wind flow. _____

Clarifying Devices 5 The function of the last paragraph is to
☐ a. give an example of a point made in the passage.
☐ b. explain a solution to a problem raised in the passage.
☐ c. show what happens when the wind blows too hard.
☐ d. show why the windmills can never work well. _____

Vocabulary in Context 6 In this passage irrigate means
☐ a. supply with water.
☐ b. cause the wind to blow.
☐ c. remove water from.
☐ d. dig trenches in. _____

Add your scores for questions 1–6. Enter the total here and on the graph on page 213.   **Total Score**   _____

64 Tilling the Soil

Early humans never tilled the soil. They merely punched a hole in the ground with a stick. A seed was then dropped into the hole. The seed was covered mainly to hide it from the birds and mice.

Much later humans found that plants grew better in loose soil. So before they dropped the seeds, they dug the soil with strong sticks, sharp stones, and clam shells. Step by step, they finally worked up to a crude plow. This plow, developed about 8,000 years ago, was a forked branch. One end was sharpened. The other end was long to hold on to. This crude plow was pulled by a farmer's children or spouse. Later, of course, oxen were used.

A big leap forward came in 1859. It happened in a field near Lancaster, England. A thousand farmers left their oxen at home to watch Guy Fawkes's great "field locomotive." Fawkes sat at the controls, gave two toots, and opened the throttle. The contraption, which looked like a monster smokestack on wheels, began to move. Ridicule turned to awe. Rapidly the machine gained speed. Soon the coal-fired steam locomotive was racing across the field faster than men could walk. And the farmers saw that it was pulling not a single "bottom," as plowmen call their plows, but eight.

Farmers couldn't believe their eyes. Fawkes plowed an acre in 12 minutes flat. Previously it would have taken a farmer an entire day to do that. Even today Fawkes's feat is amazing. Even now, with a modern tractor, a farmer allows about two-and-a-half hours for plowing an acre.

Fawkes's wonder was too big, too costly, and too hard to repair. Its great weight packed the soil too tight. It also fell into mud-holes. Thus it failed.

Main Idea	1		
		Answer	**Score**
Mark the *main idea*		M	15
Mark the statement that is *too broad*		B	5
Mark the statement that is *too narrow*		N	5
a. The crude plow has come a long way.		☐	____
b. Fawkes's field locomotive came after a long line of plowing improvements.		☐	____
c. Fawkes's steam-driven locomotive did more work in less time.		☐	____

Subject Matter   **2**   The best title for this selection would be

☐ a. The Development of Plows.

☐ b. Plowing Today.

☐ c. Ox-Drawn Plows.

☐ d. The Failure of Steam Plows.   _____

Supporting Details   **3**   Which of the following factors was **not** responsible for the failure of the steam-driven field locomotive?

☐ a. its weight

☐ b. its size

☐ c. its speed

☐ d. its price   _____

Conclusion   **4**   The author implies that today's tractors are

☐ a. larger than Fawkes's.

☐ b. easier to run.

☐ c. able to do more in less time.

☐ d. more powerful than Fawkes's.   _____

Clarifying Devices   **5**   The author uses the simile "looked like a monster smokestack on wheels" to

☐ a. show how frightened the farmers were.

☐ b. demonstrate how the plow worked.

☐ c. describe how the invention was built.

☐ d. explain how the plow looked to the farmers.   _____

Vocabulary in Context   **6**   As used in this passage, <u>contraption</u> seems to mean

☐ a. well-designed machinery.

☐ b. impressive mechanical device.

☐ c. unusual and odd-looking machine.

☐ d. useless pile of junk.   _____

Add your scores for questions 1–6. Enter the total here and on the graph on page 213.   **Total Score**   _____

65　10,000 Years of Bow and Arrow

The power of the bow was a turning point in civilization. No longer did primitive people have to face animals with club or spear. They could bring down sharp clawed beasts from a safe distance.

What the bow did for hunting, it also did for fighting. It replaced both spear and sword. Attila the Hun first showed the world the power of the bow. His Mongolian hordes swept west through Russia, Germany, and France. But the Huns were finally stopped in A.D. 451.

It was quiet for about 800 years. Then Genghis Khan decided he wanted to conquer the world. He almost did. With skilled bows, swift horses, and reckless riders, the hordes again swept westward. Russia was overrun, then Germany and Italy and even part of France. Khan's band seemed unstoppable. But the sharp sickle of disease and famine stopped it. Sick and starving, Khan's armies turned and faded into the twilight of history.

Again, it was quiet for about 200 years. Then came 1415. In Normandy, France, 13,000 English archers routed 50,000 soldiers at the famous Battle of Agincourt. How did such a small force rout such a large force? It was caused by the English longbow. This new bow was as tall as a man. With it, the English archer could shoot 6 aimed arrows in a minute. The bow could <u>propel</u> an arrow 400 yards. The French, with shorter bows, could shoot only 100 yards. You can imagine the great advantage. The English archers stood at a safe distance. They aimed their arrows high. The 13,000 archers unleashed clouds of arrows. The arrows came down on the heads of the French like rain. There was no place to hide. Those who could run turned and retreated in terror.

Main Idea	1		Answer	Score
	Mark the *main idea*		M	15
	Mark the statement that is *too broad*		B	5
	Mark the statement that is *too narrow*		N	5

a. Arrows from the longbow could travel very far. ☐ _____

b. The bow and arrow was useful in fighting. ☐ _____

c. The bow changed history with its distance, accuracy, and power. ☐ _____

Subject Matter 2 This passage focuses on the
- [ ] a. similarity between the bow and arrow.
- [ ] b. design of the bow and arrow.
- [ ] c. historic events that were affected by the bow and arrow.
- [ ] d. structure of the longbow. _____

Supporting Details 3 It is **not** true that
- [ ] a. the bow replaced the spear and sword.
- [ ] b. with skilled bows even disease could be stopped.
- [ ] c. the longbow could shoot an arrow 400 yards.
- [ ] d. the bow and arrow changed how people hunted. _____

Conclusion 4 The author feels that the bow and arrow
- [ ] a. is more violent than any other weapon.
- [ ] b. was more powerful than famine and disease.
- [ ] c. changed history forever.
- [ ] d. helped the English more than any other country. _____

Clarifying Devices 5 To help the reader understand the power of the bow and arrow, the writer uses
- [ ] a. scientific facts.
- [ ] b. famous events in history.
- [ ] c. a firsthand story.
- [ ] d. arguments and opinions. _____

Vocabulary in Context 6 The word propel means
- [ ] a. controlled motion.
- [ ] b. power.
- [ ] c. slow down.
- [ ] d. drive forward. _____

Add your scores for questions 1–6. Enter the total here and on the graph on page 213. Total Score _____

66 Discovering the Kangaroo

It was 1770. James Cook captained a British ship. His mission was to sail to New Holland, the Dutch name for Australia. (Dutch explorers got there before the English.) Australia is the only continent entirely in the Southern Hemisphere. So it made sense for it to have unusual animals.

Captain Cook landed at Botany Bay. (This is just south of present day Sydney.) He built his base there. Then he explored the <u>vast</u> inland territory. Soon he saw a strange animal. He had read about it. A Dutch captain described the animal in this way. It is about seven feet tall. It weighs about 200 pounds. Its head is like that of a deer. The ears are rabbitlike. The hind legs are powerful. Captain Cook studied the animal. It did not walk. Instead, it hopped like a grasshopper. Its powerful legs could propel it over bushes seven feet high. When chased, it leapt in 35-feet bounds. It went as fast as 35 miles per hour. But its front legs were quite tiny. It used them as a squirrel would—as hands for eating.

Captain Cook was excited to spot this strange animal. Earlier he had picked up a guide, but the guide spoke no English. So Cook used sign language. He pointed at the animal. The guide said *Kan-ga-roo.* Captain Cook wrote the word in his notebook. Some years later, missionaries came to the South Pacific islands. They listened to the natives. They wrote the sounds in English. In this way they created a written language. Now the natives could read their own spoken language. In the written language, the native word *Kan-ga-roo,* according to the dictionary, means "I don't know." Nevertheless, the animal is still called a kangaroo. The name stuck. No change is planned.

Main Idea	1			Answer	Score
		Mark the *main idea*		M	15
		Mark the statement that is *too broad*		B	5
		Mark the statement that is *too narrow*		N	5

a. Captain Cook was one of the first Europeans to see the kangaroo. ☐ _____

b. During Captain Cook's exploration he saw the kangaroo and named it. ☐ _____

c. *Kangaroo* is a native word that Captain Cook did not understand. ☐ _____

Subject Matter   **2**   This passage is about
- ☐ a. discovering Australia.
- ☐ b. discovering the kangaroo.
- ☐ c. Captain Cook's travels.
- ☐ d. the native people's language.   _____

Supporting Details   **3**   Australia was called New Holland because
- ☐ a. it was named after an explorer.
- ☐ b. explorers thought they were in Holland.
- ☐ c. the Dutch discovered the continent first.
- ☐ d. it was a new land no one had seen.   _____

Conclusion   **4**   We may conclude that the kangaroo
- ☐ a. is best known for its name.
- ☐ b. seemed unusual to Captain Cook.
- ☐ c. frightened the native people.
- ☐ d. was the largest animal the guide had ever seen.   _____

Clarifying Devices   **5**   The Dutch captain described the kangaroo by
- ☐ a. explaining its daily habits.
- ☐ b. comparing it to other animals.
- ☐ c. drawing a picture of it.
- ☐ d. listing examples.   _____

Vocabulary in Context   **6**   <u>Vast</u> means
- ☐ a. noisy.
- ☐ b. well populated.
- ☐ c. huge.
- ☐ d. tree-covered.   _____

Add your scores for questions 1–6. Enter the total here and on the graph on page 213.   **Total Score**   _____

67 Kangaroo Life

Here are some characteristics of kangaroos. The mother's pouch is shaped like a large pocket. There is where she feeds and cares for the babies. But the babies, called "joeys," are not born in the pocket. They are naturally outside it. When the babies are born, they are very tiny, only about an inch long. They must first cling to the mother's fur. Then they instinctively have to crawl up into the mother's pouch. No one helps, not even the mother. The babies must know to climb upward. They have to know there's safety in the pouch. Not only that, they have to know that that's the only way they can live. That is a lot to expect at the first minute of birth.

The babies remain in the pouch for weeks or sometimes even months. By that time, they get pretty heavy, yet the mother tolerates it. At birth there are often three kangaroos in the litter. But rarely does the mother raise more than one.

Animals in a group are referred to with special words. For cows, we say "a *herd* of cows." But what do we say for a group of kangaroos? We say "a *mob* of kangaroos."

Kangaroos live on the flat plains, where they eat grass and plants. Their teeth are very sharp. This makes it natural for them to clip the grasses close to the ground. Grass clipped so close rarely recovers; it dries up. This provokes the ranchers, as their grazing lands for cattle and sheep are often ruined. The result is that ranchers often shoot kangaroos as pests. There is, however, a use for kangaroo carcass. The flesh is considered a delicacy. The hides are used for shoes, gloves, and bags. Nevertheless, it is a shame to slaughter this <u>timid</u> animal.

Main Idea	1		
		Answer	**Score**
	Mark the *main idea*	**M**	15
	Mark the statement that is *too broad*	**B**	5
	Mark the statement that is *too narrow*	**N**	5
	a. Many people don't appreciate wild animals.	☐	_____
	b. The unusual kangaroo is often regarded as a pest.	☐	_____
	c. Kangaroos have unusual ways to care for their young.	☐	_____

Subject Matter   **2**   This passage is about
- ☐ a. the Australian countryside.
- ☐ b. ranchers.
- ☐ c. baby kangaroos.
- ☐ d. how kangaroos are born, live, and die.   _____

Supporting Details   **3**   The baby kangaroo is born
- ☐ a. outside the pouch.
- ☐ b. inside the pouch.
- ☐ c. in pockets called "joeys."
- ☐ d. with little fur.   _____

Conclusion   **4**   We can assume from the passage that shooting kangaroos is
- ☐ a. illegal.
- ☐ b. not often done.
- ☐ c. done only in restricted areas.
- ☐ d. allowed.   _____

Clarifying Devices   **5**   The writer ends this story with a
- ☐ a. new topic.
- ☐ b. personal opinion.
- ☐ c. fact.
- ☐ d. suggestion.   _____

Vocabulary in Context   **6**   The word <u>timid</u> means
- ☐ a. jumpy.
- ☐ b. sad.
- ☐ c. wild.
- ☐ d. shy.   _____

Add your scores for questions 1–6. Enter the total here and on the graph on page 213.   **Total Score**   _____

135

68 The Honeybee

Honeybees are the only insects that make food eaten by man. These bees are <u>social</u> insects. They live and work in large groups. The group or colony may contain as many as 50,000 bees. A single bee may live only a few weeks. The colony, however, may go on living for many years. The queen herself may live as long as five years. After mating with only one drone, she can lay eggs for the rest of her life. She may lay up to a million eggs in her lifetime.

Bees fly into the fields to gather food and water. They store honey to eat in winter. A worker honeybee collects nectar all day. Yet in his lifetime the nectar he collects makes less than two ounces of honey. A colony, however, can gather 25 pounds of nectar in a day.

Worker honeybees suck up nectar. Their long tongues act like straws. The bee puts the nectar into an empty cell in the hive. When the cell is full, other bees put wax caps on the cells.

Wax is produced by special glands in a bee's abdomen. The wax comes out through pores and forms tiny white flakes. The bee moves the flakes up to its jaws. It chews the wax. When the texture is just right, the wax will become part of a cell.

Beekeeping is a highly developed art. Beekeepers tend about four million hives. They gather and sell over 200 million pounds of honey each year. They also gather and sell about four million pounds of wax. One of the uses of wax is in the making of lipsticks.

Bees are useful for many things. They pollinate flowers. They also pollinate blossoms of fruit trees. Many fruits and even vegetables would die out if bees did not pollinate the blossoms.

Main Idea	1		
		Answer	**Score**
	Mark the *main idea*	M	15
	Mark the statement that is *too broad*	B	5
	Mark the statement that is *too narrow*	N	5
	a. Honeybees work together.	☐	___
	b. Colonies of bees provide both honey and wax for people.	☐	___
	c. Bees have a short life span.	☐	___

Score 15 points for each correct answer.

Subject Matter   **2**   This passage is primarily about
- ☐ a. beekeepers.
- ☐ b. wax and honey.
- ☐ c. how bees live and what they produce.
- ☐ d. why some insects live in colonies.   _____

Supporting Details   **3**   According to the author
- ☐ a. beekeepers sell more honey than wax.
- ☐ b. the hive's cells are maintained by one bee.
- ☐ c. no bee lives more than a year.
- ☐ d. a farmer profits more from bees than a beekeeper.   _____

Conclusion   **4**   From reading the passage, it is clear that bees
- ☐ a. get along better than humans.
- ☐ b. are more important to farmers' flowers than fruit trees.
- ☐ c. help fruits and vegetables grow.
- ☐ d. work harder than most insects.   _____

Clarifying Devices   **5**   The purpose of the first sentence of this passage is to
- ☐ a. get your attention.
- ☐ b. tell a story.
- ☐ c. remind you of an incident.
- ☐ d. make you upset.   _____

Vocabulary in Context   **6**   In this passage social means
- ☐ a. living in groups.
- ☐ b. friendly.
- ☐ c. talkative.
- ☐ d. large.   _____

Add your scores for questions 1–6. Enter the total here and on the graph on page 213.   Total Score   _____

69 An Unforgettable Tragedy

Here is an event that has lived in history. It is truly an unforgettable tragedy.

The event is the Fifth Crusade. This Crusade was better known as the Children's Crusade. It took place in 1212. This tragic crusade burned itself into the hearts, minds, memories, and imaginations of almost all the people in Europe. People felt bad about it for many years afterward. The reason for the long, lingering remorse might be this. Why did the parents let their children go? The Holy Land was a thousand miles away. It was held by hard-fighting Moslems. Did the parents not foresee life-and-death hardships? Did they think some magic carpet would whisk their children to the Holy Land?

This crusade was made up of young boys and girls. Many of the children were less than 12 years old. There were two armies. One was from France. The other was from Germany. None reached the Holy Land. Almost no children ever returned to their homes.

What happened to most of the children? Many died of hunger. Many died of cold weather. Fatigue took its toll. It is a long march to the Mediterranean Sea. Some did reach the sea. But it was stormy. Most children were drowned in over-loaded ships. Some reached the shore of Africa. These were captured. Then they were sold as slaves.

Some people think that this great loss of children was woven into the story of the Pied Piper of Hamelin. (The piper led the children out of the town. They were never seen again.) Like the Piper, the Crusade had a powerful drawing power. But this Piper played a tune of death.

Main Idea	1		
		Answer	**Score**
	Mark the *main idea*	M	15
	Mark the statement that is *too broad*	B	5
	Mark the statement that is *too narrow*	N	5

a. The death of young boys and girls is sad and unforgettable. ☐ _____

b. The Children's Crusade led to the tragic death of many children. ☐ _____

c. Many children in the Crusade were not even 12 years old. ☐ _____

Subject Matter   **2**   This passage is mainly about
- ☐ a. the Fourth Crusade.
- ☐ b. the Piper's Crusade.
- ☐ c. crusades.
- ☐ d. the Fifth Crusade.   _____

Supporting Details   **3**   According to the passage, all of the following are true about the Crusade except that
- ☐ a. parents wanted their children to live in a new country.
- ☐ b. the armies were from France and Germany.
- ☐ c. the children did not reach the Holy Land.
- ☐ d. children drowned in crowded ships.   _____

Conclusion   **4**   It is clear from this passage that the author does not
- ☐ a. like the Pied Piper story.
- ☐ b. understand how parents could let their children leave.
- ☐ c. know what happened to the children in the Crusade.
- ☐ d. enjoy reading about history.   _____

Clarifying Devices   **5**   The writer uses the word "but" in the last paragraph to indicate
- ☐ a. a contradiction.
- ☐ b. an exception.
- ☐ c. an argument.
- ☐ d. a comparison.   _____

Vocabulary in Context   **6**   Fatigue means
- ☐ a. distance.
- ☐ b. sadness.
- ☐ c. exhaustion.
- ☐ d. loneliness.   _____

Add your scores for questions 1–6. Enter the total here and on the graph on page 213.

Total Score   _____

70 Ancient Firefighting

Fire is both a friend and a foe. It is a friend when under control. It is a foe when out of control.

Long ago, people found that fire could be put out by throwing water on it. This worked well when people lived some distance apart. But when people moved into towns, their houses were usually side by side. This closeness created a problem. Now a burning house was a danger to all.

The problem was soon solved. If a fire broke out, people quickly formed a line. The line led from a pond or well to the house that was on fire. Buckets of water were passed along the line.

With the passing of time, another problem arose. The buildings became bigger. With bigger buildings, you had bigger flames. These flames flared out. Now the firefighters could not get close enough to the burning building to throw the water from the buckets on it. How did they solve this problem? Old records give us a glimpse.

This may sound surprising. Fire equipment goes back to the time of Christ. Caesar Augustus (63 B.C.–A.D. 14) formed the first fire department in Rome. Seven hundred firefighters lived in firehouses throughout the city. They used a wheeled chariot that squirted water on fires. This "water squirt" was a huge <u>syringe</u>. The bulb may have been as long as a man's body. It was squeezed by means of a giant screw turned by a firefighter. Such squirts were also used when the Great Fire swept London in 1666. Hand syringes three feet long were also used. These squirts were held by two firefighters while a third worked the plunger.

It took the London fire to awaken people to the need for better equipment.

Main Idea   1

	Answer	Score
Mark the *main idea*	M	15
Mark the statement that is *too broad*	B	5
Mark the statement that is *too narrow*	N	5

a. Water squirts were used to fight the Great Fire in London in 1666. ☐ _____

b. Methods for fighting fires have improved as the need arose. ☐ _____

c. Fires in places where people live can be dangerous. ☐ _____

Subject Matter 2 This passage is mostly about
☐ a. firefighters.
☐ b. Caesar Augustus.
☐ c. the Great Fire of London.
☐ d. the development of firefighting techniques.   _____

Supporting Details 3 Which of the following is **not** true?
☐ a. The water squirt was used only in Rome.
☐ b. A water squirt is a huge syringe.
☐ c. Caesar Augustus formed the first fire department in Rome.
☐ d. Firefighting techniques developed before the time of Christ.   _____

Conclusion 4 From this passage you can conclude that during the time of Caesar Augustus
☐ a. people considered firefighting unimportant.
☐ b. people wanted to prevent forest fires.
☐ c. there were no fires in Rome.
☐ d. many lives were saved from fire.   _____

Clarifying Devices 5 In the final paragraph the author uses which of the following methods?
☐ a. comparison
☐ b. direct quote
☐ c. personal opinion
☐ d. argumentative statement   _____

Vocabulary in Context 6 As used in this passage a <u>syringe</u> is a
☐ a. water pail.
☐ b. kind of vacuum cleaner.
☐ c. a hose.
☐ d. tube with a valve that can collect and shoot out liquids.   _____

Add your scores for questions 1–6. Enter the total here and on the graph on page 213.   **Total Score**   _____

141

71 Basketball

Who invented basketball? Most people know the answer. It's James A. Naismith. Naismith was an instructor in physical education. He worked at a YMCA training school in Massachusetts. (Later this became Springfield College.) His goal was to provide an indoor sport for the winter.

Naismith <u>conceived</u> the game of basketball in 1891. He formed the basic rules. He asked the janitor to nail two boxes at each end of a gym. The janitor could only find some round half-bushel baskets. He nailed these to the balconies at each end. Players used a soccer ball. The object of the game was to put the ball into the basket. Thus, we have *basketball.*

The half-bushel baskets had fixed bottoms. When the ball went into the basket, there was a problem. A ladder had to be used to get the ball out. Soon metal baskets with bottoms replaced the wooden ones. These baskets had a small hole in the bottom. A pole was used to poke the ball out. The next improvement: the metal basket now had a closed net attached. Now the official pulled a cord attached to the net. The ball then would drop down. In about 1913, the bottomless baskets came into use. You wonder why it took so long. But getting the ball out of the baskets was not such a big job. The scores were low. A typical score for a full game might be 19 to 17.

Backboards were introduced in 1894. Before that, spectators would lean over balconies, blocking shots. The soccer ball was also replaced that year. The new ball came in two parts. The outer covering was leather. The inner part was a rubber bladder. The opening was laced. The laceless ball came into use in 1937. The molded ball of today became official in only 1950.

Main Idea	1	Answer	Score
	Mark the *main idea*	M	15
	Mark the statement that is *too broad*	B	5
	Mark the statement that is *too narrow*	N	5

a.	Half-bushel baskets were replaced with metal ones.	☐ ____
b.	Over time, basketball has changed.	☐ ____
c.	As basketball developed, many improvements were introduced.	☐ ____

Subject Matter   **2**   The best alternate title for this passage would be
- ☐ a. From Soccer Balls to Basketballs.
- ☐ b. The Inventor of the Basketball.
- ☐ c. Change Is Hard.
- ☐ d. Naismith and Indoor Sports.   _____

Supporting Details   **3**   James A. Naismith was
- ☐ a. a college basketball coach.
- ☐ b. the creator of the metal basket.
- ☐ c. the inventor of basketball.
- ☐ d. a YMCA executive.   _____

Conclusion   **4**   This passage suggests that
- ☐ a. basketball is a great indoor sport.
- ☐ b. the rules Naismith formed have not changed.
- ☐ c. metal baskets were the greatest improvement made.
- ☐ d. the pace of early games was rather slow.   _____

Clarifying Devices   **5**   The author explains how basketball developed by
- ☐ a. telling about early players.
- ☐ b. giving examples.
- ☐ c. describing early basketball games.
- ☐ d. comparing the past with the present.   _____

Vocabulary in Context   **6**   As used in this passage, the word <u>conceived</u> means
- ☐ a. started to understand.
- ☐ b. created.
- ☐ c. copied.
- ☐ d. organized.   _____

Add your scores for questions 1–6. Enter the total here and on the graph on page 213.   **Total Score**   _____

72 The Migration of Birds

Birds are lucky. They can chirp, "Have wings. Will travel." Birds migrate for various reasons. But mainly it's the food supply.

How do birds find their way? A partial answer: They follow such landmarks as coastlines. Some birds fly inland routes. Perhaps they follow rivers or mountain ranges. But some birds fly only at night. Then landmarks are of little use. There is still much to learn about migration.

Great distances are covered during migrations. The arctic tern holds the record. It flies 22,000 miles roundtrip. It leaves the Arctic Circle in late August. Its destination is the Antarctic Circle. Later, the terns fly north. They arrive at the Arctic Circle about mid-June.

The tern may hold the record, but the bobolink is competing. Bobolinks fly in one big flock. Their route is called the bobolink route. Few other birds ever use it. Flying only at night, they leave the island of Jamaica and fly 500 miles over the ocean nonstop to Mexico.

But the hummingbird is the real wonder bird. It may fly from the eastern United States over the Gulf of Mexico to the Yucatan in Mexico. How can such a small bird have enough energy to fly such a distance nonstop? This bird is the smallest and daintiest one in the U.S. It is less than four inches long. It lives on nectar from flowers. This nectar provides the power to its wings. The wings move about 60 to 70 times a second (not minute). You can be sure of this: there are no flower refueling stations on the gulf. There are no islands. Some speculate the birds get into air currents. But nobody really knows. It's a mystery. It's a wonder. It's good to still have wonders.

Main Idea	1	Answer	Score
Mark the *main idea*		M	15
Mark the statement that is *too broad*		B	5
Mark the statement that is *too narrow*		N	5

a. Birds travel great distances and fly interesting routes when they migrate. ☐ _____

b. The migration of birds is an amazing mystery. ☐ _____

c. Birds may follow landmarks such as coastlines during migration. ☐ _____

Subject Matter   **2**   The subject of this passage is
☐ a. the bird that travels the farthest.
☐ b. birds' landmarks.
☐ c. birds' migration patterns.
☐ d. the greatest distance covered during migration.   _____

Supporting
Details   **3**   Arctic terns
☐ a. are the smallest bird.
☐ b. only fly at night.
☐ c. fly to Mexico.
☐ d. migrate to the Arctic Circle.   _____

Conclusion   **4**   Based on some of the routes they fly, it is clear that
☐ a. some birds can travel nonstop without eating.
☐ b. the smallest bird has the most energy.
☐ c. birds sleep on the surface of water.
☐ d. some birds enjoy migration more than others.   _____

Clarifying
Devices   **5**   The last sentence indicates that the author
☐ a. will continue to research this subject.
☐ b. is annoyed no one has all the answers
about migration.
☐ c. likes wondering about nature.
☐ d. likes the hummingbird the most of all the
birds.   _____

Vocabulary
in Context   **6**   To <u>speculate</u> means to
☐ a. know.
☐ b. see.
☐ c. guess.
☐ d. agree.   _____

Add your scores for questions 1–6. Enter the total here   **Total**
and on the graph on page 213.   **Score**   _____

73 Riding the Desert Camel

Mention camel, and we quickly think of the desert—usually the Sahara Desert of North Africa. But did you know that the camel was native first to North America? This was 40,000,000 years ago. The camel probably got to Africa by migrating to South America. This was a large land mass that broke in two. The eastern part we now call Africa. The journey took millions of years.

Camels stand six to seven feet tall and weigh up to 1,600 pounds. They have long, strong legs and powerful muscles. A camel can carry as much as a thousand pounds for a short distance. But for long distances, its typical load is about 400 pounds.

When a camel walks or runs, both legs on one side of its body move forward at the same time. Then the legs on the other side swing forward. This leg action makes for a swaying, rocking motion. Some riders get "seasick." This may be part of the reason that camels are sometimes called "ships of the desert."

A camel's back is broad. It is too broad to let both of the rider's feet hang down. There is no use for stirrups. Well, then, how do you ride a camel? Camel drivers teach you to wrap one leg around the tall saddle horn. Then tuck the foot beneath the other leg. Let this leg just dangle. Or you can wrap both legs around the horn and sit cross-legged.

As for your hands, you can hold the reins gently. But if the going gets rough, you can clutch the saddle horn in desperation. Once you get used to the camel's constant rocking gait, though, you can almost be <u>lulled</u> to sleep.

Main Idea   1

	Answer	Score
Mark the *main idea*	M	15
Mark the statement that is *too broad*	B	5
Mark the statement that is *too narrow*	N	5

a. The camel is tall and strong, but it is not too easy to ride. ☐ _____

b. The camel moves both legs on one side of its body together. ☐ _____

c. The camel offers a somewhat unusual ride. ☐ _____

Score 15 points for each correct answer.   **Score**

Subject Matter   **2**   The author's main point is that riding a camel
- ☐ a. demands strength.
- ☐ b. is impossible.
- ☐ c. requires one to be experienced.
- ☐ d. is dangerous.   _____

Supporting   **3**   According to information in the passage, which
Details   of these statements is **not** true?
- ☐ a. There are no stirrups to assist the camel rider.
- ☐ b. Camels have a wider back than horses.
- ☐ c. Sitting cross-legged is not a good way to ride a camel.
- ☐ d. The camel's rocking motion is made from its long leg action.   _____

Conclusion   **4**   We can conclude that a camel rider is supposed to
- ☐ a. practice to get used to the ride.
- ☐ b. sleep while riding.
- ☐ c. watch the camel drivers.
- ☐ d. use only one comfortable position.   _____

Clarifying   **5**   The content of this paragraph can best be
Devices   described as
- ☐ a. an argument.
- ☐ b. a personal memory.
- ☐ c. a comparison.
- ☐ d. informative.   _____

Vocabulary   **6**   As used in the paragraph, <u>lulled</u> most nearly means
in Context
- ☐ a. sung to.
- ☐ b. soothed.
- ☐ c. shaken.
- ☐ d. shocked.   _____

Add your scores for questions 1–6. Enter the total here   **Total**
and on the graph on page 213.   **Score**   _____

74 A Line on Kites

Kites are sources of childhood fun. But did you know that not all kites were used as toys?

In 1752 Ben Franklin used a kite to prove that lightning and electricity are the same. He made a flat kite. Then he tied a piece of iron wire to it. This he knew would attract the lightning. Next he used a ball of hemp string. At the end of the string he tied a long silk ribbon. The ribbon would serve as a protective insulator. Between the string and the ribbon he attached a brass key.

The kite rose into a dark cloud. Soon the rain-wet string began to stiffen. It bristled as if it were alive. Franklin knew electricity was <u>coursing</u> down the string. He put his finger near the key. A series of sparks jumped from key to finger. He felt the sharp tingle of the sparks. These were really electrical shocks. Franklin's experiment was dangerous. It took great courage.

Others experimented with kites too. In 1749, two Scotsmen tied a thermometer to a kite. They recorded the temperature of the clouds. Then in 1883, two Englishmen tied a wind meter to a kite. The speed of the wind was measured at 1,200 feet.

The suspension bridge at Niagara Falls was begun by a kite. The kite carried a light line over the gorge. Then the light line drew a heavier one across. Finally, a steel cable was pulled over.

This next event made world history. In 1901, Guglielmo Marconi wanted to prove that a radio signal could be sent across the Atlantic. But first he had to overcome the curve of the earth. He had a brilliant idea. In Newfoundland, he had the receiving antenna raised high in the air on the tail of a kite. The signal came over the Atlantic loud and clear.

Main Idea	1	Answer	Score
	Mark the *main idea*	M	15
	Mark the statement that is *too broad*	B	5
	Mark the statement that is *too narrow*	N	5

a. Kites have been useful in many historic discoveries. ☐ _____

b. Kites have made people famous. ☐ _____

c. The kite proved electricity and lightning are the same. ☐ _____

Subject Matter   **2**   In this passage the author tries to
- [ ] a. explain why kites are popular.
- [ ] b. give an explanation of how kites work.
- [ ] c. describe how kites have been important in the past.
- [ ] d. define various ways we can use kites.   _____

Supporting Details   **3**   Benjamin Franklin used a flat kite to
- [ ] a. prove that lightning was electricity.
- [ ] b. make electricity.
- [ ] c. show how lightning is dangerous.
- [ ] d. demonstrate his courage.   _____

Conclusion   **4**   We can conclude from this passage that kites
- [ ] a. are better to use for experiments than for play.
- [ ] b. come in many shapes and sizes.
- [ ] c. have more than one purpose.
- [ ] d. are enjoyed by famous people.   _____

Clarifying Devices   **5**   The opening sentence of the final paragraph is intended to
- [ ] a. point out a contrast.
- [ ] b. attract your attention.
- [ ] c. end an exciting story.
- [ ] d. prove a point.   _____

Vocabulary in Context   **6**   Another word for <u>coursing</u> might be
- [ ] a. stopping.
- [ ] b. leading.
- [ ] c. moving.
- [ ] d. following.   _____

Add your scores for questions 1–6. Enter the total here and on the graph on page 213.   **Total Score**   _____

75 The Flying Penguin

Penguins are great swimmers. They are better than many other totally aquatic creatures. Penguins are really birds. But they cannot fly. They lost that ability millions of years ago. Their wings developed into flippers. Now the flippers serve as paddles in the water. Penguins once also had regular bird feet. But over millions of years, the feet became webbed. The flippers and the webbed feet make penguins swift swimmers and deep divers.

Why the change from a flying to a swimming bird? Scientists only guess. It may have been a need for food. There was nothing else available, so penguins constantly dove into schools of fish.

Then another great change took place. Nature equipped the penguin's body with built-in "shock absorbers." These are feathers that grow straight out from the body and then toward their ends take a right-angled turn. Why does the penguin need these? After dining in the water, the bird has a problem. It needs to get back on top of an ice floe. The floes are some five or six feet above the water. Here's what the penguin does. It swims in close. It measures the height of the floe with a watery eye. It turns and heads out some 30 feet. Then it turns toward the floe and races at top speed under water. Scientists have clocked its speed to about 60 miles per hour.

Now, here's the tricky part. Just short of the ice floe, the penguin planes upwards and becomes a hurtling aerial torpedo. Most of the time, a penguin will make it to the top of the ice floe. But on occasion, it smacks hard into the icy side of the floe. The impact would be hard enough to cripple the penguin or even kill it. But the <u>ingenious</u> feather "shock absorbers" save it.

Main Idea	1		
		Answer	**Score**
	Mark the *main idea*	M	15
	Mark the statement that is *too broad*	B	5
	Mark the statement that is *too narrow*	N	5

a. Penguins are well-adapted to aquatic life. ☐ _____

b. The penguin's flippers were once wings. ☐ _____

c. The penguin is a swimming bird. ☐ _____

Score 15 points for each correct answer.   **Score**

Subject Matter   **2** This passage deals mainly with
- ☐ a. dangerous ice floes.
- ☐ b. the eating habits of the penguin.
- ☐ c. swimming birds.
- ☐ d. the penguin as a creature of the water.   _____

Supporting   **3** Penguins can swim
Details
- ☐ a. up the side of an ice floe.
- ☐ b. almost as well as they can fly.
- ☐ c. up to 60 miles per hour.
- ☐ d. because of their built-in shock absorbers.   _____

Conclusion   **4** We can infer from the article that penguins are
- ☐ a. often killed by hitting ice floes.
- ☐ b. able to measure distances under water.
- ☐ c. protected from impacts by their feathers.
- ☐ d. similar to porpoises.   _____

Clarifying   **5** The author makes a comparison between the
Devices   penguin and a torpedo in order to
- ☐ a. explain the size of the penguin.
- ☐ b. describe how dangerous its movement can be.
- ☐ c. explain how the penguin swims.
- ☐ d. help us imagine the penguin's speed.   _____

Vocabulary   **6** The word <u>ingenious</u>, as used in the passage, means
in Context
- ☐ a. clever.
- ☐ b. useful.
- ☐ c. candid.
- ☐ d. imitation.   _____

Add your scores for questions 1–6. Enter the total here   **Total**
and on the graph on page 213.   **Score**   _____

76 Courage and Nobility

It was September of 1862. General Robert E. Lee marched into Maryland. He led 50,000 troops. Lee's best officer, Stonewall Jackson, was there too. He rode at the head of his troops into the town of Frederick.

In the morning 40 Union flags graced the town. Each owner quickly hauled his down. They heard the tramping of feet and the striking of hooves. The streets were empty now. Everyone was hiding behind shuttered windows. But one old woman did not hide. Barbara Frietchie took out her flag and hung it from her attic window.

Stonewall Jackson, riding ahead, spied the flag. The order "FIRE!" brought a shattering of glass and splintering of wood. As the broken staff was cracking and falling, a wrinkled old hand reached out. Barbara Frietchie caught the flag, now tattered and filled with holes. According to legend, this is what she said:

> Shoot, if you must, this old gray head,
> But spare your country's flag.

Riding below, Jackson heard her words. He was a brave and noble man. He must also have been impressed with the old woman's bravery and nobility. He turned to his troops. He ordered them to stop shooting. Barbara Frietchie was unharmed.

Frietchie's house still stands. The one-and-a-half-story brick building is in Frederick. Her clothing, her spinning wheel, her Bible are still waiting. And a flag hangs over her house.

Main Idea 1		Answer	Score
Mark the *main idea*		M	15
Mark the statement that is *too broad*		B	5
Mark the statement that is *too narrow*		N	5

a. Barbara Frietchie's bravery and loyalty were recognized by Stonewall Jackson. ☐ _____

b. Stonewall Jackson ordered his soldiers to stop shooting. ☐ _____

c. Barbara Frietchie bravely faced the enemy. ☐ _____

Score 15 points for each correct answer.   **Score**

Subject Matter   **2**   This main purpose of this passage is to
☐ a. describe the life of Barbara Frietchie.
☐ b. show how courage and spirit were needed in the 1800s.
☐ c. tell an important episode in Barbara Frietchie's life.
☐ d. explain people's feelings during the Civil War.   _____

Supporting Details   **3**   Despite Barbara Frietchie's old age she
☐ a. convinced Stonewall Jackson to leave town.
☐ b. stood firm in her beliefs.
☐ c. had strong opinions that war was evil.
☐ d. spoke loudly.   _____

Conclusion   **4**   Which of the following is most likely true?
☐ a. Frederick has many mementos of the Civil War.
☐ b. Jackson was scolded by General Lee.
☐ c. The Confederates made no raids after Frederick.
☐ d. The townspeople were embarrassed by Frietchie.   _____

Clarifying Devices   **5**   The last sentence of the story suggests that
☐ a. people in Frederick live in the past.
☐ b. people remember what Frietchie did.
☐ c. people in Frederick love flags.
☐ d. Stonewall Jackson never came to Frederick again.   _____

Vocabulary in Context   **6**   In this passage, <u>spied</u> means
☐ a. spotted.
☐ b. sneaked.
☐ c. surprised.
☐ d. held.   _____

Add your scores for questions 1–6. Enter the total here and on the graph on page 214.   **Total Score**   _____

77 The Faithful Dog

Which animal is "man's best friend"? We all know it's the dog. Dogs have earned the love and respect of humans. Many have given their own lives to save people. Dogs are faithful and devoted. For example Bobby, a Skye terrier, went to market with his Scottish master every day. After the man died, Bobby would not move from his grave. He stayed there for about 10 years. He stayed until he died.

Dogs serve many useful functions. They are good at watching and herding sheep. Wherever sheep are raised, a sheep-herding dog is developed. For instance, there is the German Shepherd dog. In Scotland, there is the Shetland sheep dog. Both are recognized breeds.

Specially trained dogs lead the blind. Such dogs are carefully selected. It takes about three to five months to train them. Guide dogs will refuse to cross a busy street unless the traffic has stopped.

One interesting dog is the St. Bernard. How did it get its name? It was developed by the monks of the St. Bernard Monastery. This is located in the Alps of Switzerland. The dog weighs from 140 to 220 pounds. It's one of the heaviest of all dogs.

St. Bernards are famous for rescuing travelers lost in the snow. They have a wonderful sense of smell. They find people buried under several feet of snow. A St. Bernard named Barry rescued 40 persons. This was over a period of years.

There is a popular <u>misconception</u> about these dogs. They do not carry flasks around their necks. Sir Edwin Landseer misrepresented them this way in a painting.

Main Idea	1	Answer	Score
	Mark the *main idea*	M	15
	Mark the statement that is *too broad*	B	5
	Mark the statement that is *too narrow*	N	5

		Answer	Score
a.	Many animals have been trained to work for humans.	☐	_____
b.	The Saint Bernard is known for finding lost people.	☐	_____
c.	Dogs are not only loyal companions but can also be helpful.	☐	_____

Subject Matter   **2**   This passage is mainly about
- ☐ a. friendly dogs.
- ☐ b. breeds of dogs.
- ☐ c. useful dogs.
- ☐ d. small dogs.   _____

Supporting Details   **3**   Dogs trained to lead the blind are
- ☐ a. Saint Bernards.
- ☐ b. chosen very carefully.
- ☐ c. trained for seven to 10 months.
- ☐ d. raised around blind people.   _____

Conclusion   **4**   The dog named Bobby can best be described as
- ☐ a. lost.
- ☐ b. tired.
- ☐ c. loyal.
- ☐ d. friendly.   _____

Clarifying Devices   **5**   To tell this story the author depends mainly on
- ☐ a. stories from dog trainers.
- ☐ b. lists of different kinds of dogs.
- ☐ c. stories about specific dog breeds.
- ☐ d. detailed descriptions of various dogs.   _____

Vocabulary in Context   **6**   The word <u>misconception</u> means something that is
- ☐ a. well stated.
- ☐ b. not correctly understood.
- ☐ c. a personal belief.
- ☐ d. confusing.   _____

Add your scores for questions 1–6. Enter the total here and on the graph on page 214.   Total Score   _____

78 Olympics and the Marathon

Records show that the first Olympic games were held in 776 B.C. Scholars, however, believe the games began hundreds of years before. They base this belief on slim clues on some old scrolls.

The games were not played continuously since 776 B.C. They were stopped in A.D. 394 because they became <u>corrupt</u>. The best athletes were not chosen. Choices were political. Even Emperor Nero entered, and he was no athlete. So the Olympics were not played for 1,500 years. Then a lucky thing happened. A group found ruins of the ancient Olympic stadium in 1878.

News spread. A rich French baron became interested. And in 1896 the games were renewed. The baron insisted that the marathon race be added. After all, he argued, the run from Marathon saved Athens and perhaps all of Greece. Here is that story.

The battle of Marathon took place in 490 B.C. A runner was sent to carry the news of victory to the army at Athens. The runner was a soldier named Pheidippides. He reported the victory. Then, exhausted, he dropped dead. He had run 22 miles and 1,470 yards. The distance was measured up to the high pile of brave dead. This spot is still marked.

But wait. Isn't the marathon 26 miles and 385 yards? Yes. But game by game, the distance varied. It was usually around 24 miles. The present length was finally set in 1924. Here is how it was agreed on. The Olympics of 1908 had been held in London. The starting line was at the royal residence at Windsor Castle. The goal was the stadium. This was exactly 26 miles. But the finishing line was extended 385 yards so that the race would end in front of the royal box.

Main Idea 1

	Answer	Score
Mark the *main idea*	M	15
Mark the statement that is *too broad*	B	5
Mark the statement that is *too narrow*	N	5

a. The Olympics have been played for hundreds of years. ☐ _____

b. The distance of the marathon was originally based on Pheidippides' run. ☐ _____

c. The Olympics and the marathon started years ago and developed through the years. ☐ _____

Score 15 points for each correct answer.   Score

Subject Matter   **2**   The first paragraph lets us know that this passage
is about
☐ a. the history of the Olympics.
☐ b. life when the Olympic games began.
☐ c. keeping records on history.
☐ d. today's Olympics.   _____

Supporting   **3**   The marathon was added to the Olympic games
Details   because
☐ a. there was a great runner named Pheidippides.
☐ b. a French nobleman introduced the idea.
☐ c. a soldier ran 22 miles to carry a message.
☐ d. running had not yet been included in the
games.   _____

Conclusion   **4**   One could conclude from this passage that
☐ a. there are records showing how other
Olympic traditions began.
☐ b. Olympics in the past were not well organized.
☐ c. English royalty have always been strong
Olympic supporters.
☐ d. people and politics have always affected the
Olympics.   _____

Clarifying   **5**   The author presents the information by
Devices   ☐ a. using precise dates and time.
☐ b. telling about events from the past.
☐ c. using the opinions of historians.
☐ d. giving a list of details.   _____

Vocabulary   **6**   In this passage <u>corrupt</u> means
in Context   ☐ a. stopped.
☐ b. unorganized.
☐ c. difficult.
☐ d. dishonest.   _____

Add your scores for questions 1–6. Enter the total here   **Total**
and on the graph on page 214.   **Score**   _____

79 The Man Who Planted Apple Trees

Does the name John Chapman ring a bell? Most people would answer no. But many people would have heard of Johnny Appleseed. Here is some information about the man.

Johnny was born in Massachusetts. He was born in 1774 and died in about 1845. He probably died in the wilderness. He is always pictured there. This is why he seemed like an American version of a prophet. Like a prophet, he tried to get people to listen to him.

And people did listen. But Johnny did more than just talk. He carried a bushel of apple seeds on his back. He also carried in his arms bundles of young apple tree sprouts. He planted them in open spots where the sun could shine on them. He planted them in open fields too. He planted them on the lands of settlers. He planted them on the lands of the Indians. Year after year, people ate the apples from his trees. They even dried the apples in the sun for winter's food.

Johnny was more than just a nurseryman. He was a medicine man too. He knew the healing power of herbs. He often helped settlers with boneset. This is a flowering plant that grows wild in meadows. When used as a tea, it reduces fevers. It helps broken bones heal faster too.

Johnny was also a military hero. The War of 1812 was raging. Lake Erie was a stronghold of the British. Johnny knew the Ohio River. He also knew northern Ohio. He carried precious messages between American commanders. He knew every path, trail, stream, and river. But Johnny was a true apple seed to the end. It is nice to think that he died gently placing soil around the tender roots of his last apple tree.

Main Idea	1		Answer	Score
	Mark the *main idea*		M	15
	Mark the statement that is *too broad*		B	5
	Mark the statement that is *too narrow*		N	5

a. Apple trees now grow over much of the United States. ☐ _____

b. No one knows how Johnny Appleseed died. ☐ _____

c. Johnny Appleseed lived in the wilderness planting seeds and helping others. ☐ _____

Score 15 points for each correct answer.   **Score**

Subject Matter 　2　This passage is about Johnny Appleseed's
- ☐ a. personality.
- ☐ b. kindness.
- ☐ c. life.
- ☐ d. folktale.

_____

Supporting
Details 　　　　3　Johnny Appleseed not only planted seeds; he also
- ☐ a. picked apples.
- ☐ b. grew flowers.
- ☐ c. worked in medicine.
- ☐ d. fought in the War of 1812.

_____

Conclusion 　　4　We can assume from the passage that the author
- ☐ a. likes apples.
- ☐ b. knows many stories.
- ☐ c. believes Johnny Appleseed was special.
- ☐ d. was a great-grandchild of Johnny Appleseed.

_____

Clarifying
Devices 　　　　5　What does the author mean by "But Johnny was
a true apple seed to the end"?
- ☐ a. He died planting seeds and rests among the apple tree roots.
- ☐ b. Until he died, he cared more about apple trees than anything else.
- ☐ c. He was buried like an apple seed.
- ☐ d. At the end he looked small, like an apple seed.

_____

Vocabulary
in Context 　　6　The word <u>stronghold</u>, as used in this passage, means a
- ☐ a. tight fit.
- ☐ b. safe, well-protected place.
- ☐ c. way to travel.
- ☐ d. site of a small fort.

_____

Add your scores for questions 1–6. Enter the total here　**Total**
and on the graph on page 214.　　　　　　　　　　　　**Score**

_____

80 Rudolph's Rugged Relatives

Where do you find the country of Lapland on the map? You don't. Lapland is not a separate country. It is just a large area north of the Arctic Circle where the Lapp people live. They live in sections that belong to Norway, Sweden, Finland, and Russia. The Lapps have no government of their own. They are governed by the country in whose area they live. These countries have respect for the Lapps' unique culture. They leave them to develop very much on their own lines.

Lapland is a bleak, barren region. The birches, pines, and firs that somehow survive are thin, bent by the wind, and stunted. The cold is intense and the growing season is very short. For three months, the sun never rises. For another three months, the sun never sets. About 34,000 people live in the region. The people look somewhat like Chinese or Japanese. Their average height is about five feet. However, they are strong and muscular.

Lapps originally came from east of the Urals in Russia. The Finns followed them. Being more advanced, they forced the Lapps farther and farther north. The Lapps found safety and peace in the icy northern wastes. In their own language they call themselves "the <u>banished</u>."

Lapp survival is tied entirely to a thick growth of mosses and lichens. The Lapps do not eat this growth. But reindeer do. They get strong and fat on this "grass" of the far north. The entire village folds its reindeer-skin tents and follows the herd's northward trek. As winter approaches and the snows begin, the herds stop, turn, and slowly head south. The village follows the herd. This cycle has been repeated for thousands of years. Will it be repeated for yet thousands more?

Main Idea 1

	Answer	Score
Mark the *main idea*	M	15
Mark the statement that is *too broad*	B	5
Mark the statement that is *too narrow*	N	5

a. The Lapps follow reindeer herds as they move to new areas. ☐ _____

b. The Lapps are people of the Far North. ☐ _____

c. Lapland and its people have developed as a unique culture. ☐ _____

Score 15 points for each correct answer.   **Score**

Subject Matter   **2**   The subject of this passage is
- ☐ a. reindeer.
- ☐ b. the Arctic Circle.
- ☐ c. a nation of people.
- ☐ d. primitive people.

_____

Supporting Details   **3**   Reindeer are important to the Lapps because they
- ☐ a. protect them.
- ☐ b. eat unwanted grasses.
- ☐ c. provide food and shelter.
- ☐ d. lead villagers to new areas.

_____

Conclusion   **4**   After reading this passage, we can guess that
- ☐ a. Lapp clothing is made from reindeer skin.
- ☐ b. the Lapps celebrate winter holidays.
- ☐ c. Lapland is a dark and unfriendly place.
- ☐ d. herds of reindeer make living in Lapland difficult.

_____

Clarifying Devices   **5**   The author mentions the migration of Finns in order to explain the Lapps'
- ☐ a. racial connection to them.
- ☐ b. dependence on reindeer.
- ☐ c. reasons for living so far north.
- ☐ d. primitive culture.

_____

Vocabulary in Context   **6**   The word <u>banished</u> as used in this passage is closest in meaning to
- ☐ a. hopeless.
- ☐ b. lonesome.
- ☐ c. sent away.
- ☐ d. scared.

_____

Add your scores for questions 1–6. Enter the total here and on the graph on page 214.   **Total Score**

_____

81 The Steamship *Savannah*

Steamboats on rivers were a success. They easily plied the calm waters. But could they take the battering of a rough ocean? This question was put to the test in 1819.

The American packet ship, the *Savannah,* was planning to steam across the Atlantic. The *Savannah* was a 110-foot ship. It was not newly built. It was converted. It was a full-rigged sailing ship. It was simply refitted. A steam engine was added to power two side paddle wheels.

The *Savannah* left New York City on May 22, 1819. It docked at Liverpool, England, on June 20. The journey was made in 29 days. During the trip, the ship ran its engine only 85 hours. After that, the fuel was used up. The rest of the trip was made using sails. The *Savannah* returned to the United States under sail alone. The engine was not used. Nevertheless, the *Savannah* is in the records as the first steamship to cross the Atlantic.

Another steamship also crossed the Atlantic, in 1838. It was the British ship, the *Sirius*. It used steam power all the way. It was also a side-wheeler. The trip took $18^1/_2$ days.

These trips revealed one serious weakness. It was with the large side-wheels. The waves battered these rather fragile devices mercilessly. Something had to replace them. But what? The solution was the propeller. It was wholly under water at a ship's stern. It used power more <u>efficiently</u>.

The steamship the *Great Britain* was designed in 1845. It became the first propeller-driven ship to travel across the Atlantic.

Main Idea	1			
			Answer	**Score**
	Mark the *main idea*		[M]	15
	Mark the statement that is *too broad*		[B]	5
	Mark the statement that is *too narrow*		[N]	5

a. The success of the steamship led to the *Savannah* and other ships crossing the Atlantic Ocean. ☐ _____

b. Steamships became the popular way to travel in the 1800s. ☐ _____

c. The *Savannah* made its trip across the Atlantic using its steam engine and its sails. ☐ _____

Subject Matter | **2** | This selection centers on
☐ a. the first steamship.
☐ b. ocean-crossing steamships.
☐ c. the *Savannah* crossing the Atlantic.
☐ d. traveling by water.   _____

Supporting Details | **3** | The *Savannah*
☐ a. had two paddle wheels.
☐ b. had two sails.
☐ c. was the first steamship.
☐ d. only used its engine.   _____

Conclusion | **4** | From this passage, it appears that the steamship
☐ a. was the only way to travel.
☐ b. allowed people to travel to other countries.
☐ c. replaced sailboats.
☐ d. brought goods as well as people to the United States.   _____

Clarifying Devices | **5** | Most of the passage is devoted to
☐ a. facts and statistics.
☐ b. a story.
☐ c. opinions of famous people.
☐ d. personal experiences.   _____

Vocabulary in Context | **6** | Something done <u>efficiently</u> is done
☐ a. very quickly.
☐ b. slowly.
☐ c. with lots of work.
☐ d. with little effort.   _____

**Add your scores for questions 1–6. Enter the total here
and on the graph on page 214.**   **Total
Score**   _____

82 The Test of All Tests

You have read about the Arabian horse. It was developed by the Arabs for use in the desert. It was bred to function under some of the harshest conditions in the world. Centuries of patient breeding were needed. Bloodlines were passed on from generation to generation of breeders.

The armies of Arabia used the horse for combat. (Camels were used for patrol duty.) Horses were chosen with great care. Over months, they were put through one test after another. One test was to respond to the ear-piercing sounds of an ancient Arabian horn. The sound had to pierce the din and <u>tumult</u> of battle. The horn of battle was used in the final, most important test.

For this final test, the horses were put into a strong wooden corral. The corral was at the top of a long, sloping hill. At the bottom of the hill was a freshwater lake. The horses were not fed, nor were they given any water. Horses became almost crazed with thirst. They threw themselves at the logged corral and tried to break out. The corral was much too high to jump. Finally, the horses were judged to be at the breaking point. Then the broad gates suddenly swung open. The herd exploded out of the corral. They practically flew down the slope. Their nostrils were smelling and their tongues "tasting" the water. The trainers watched intently. Before the first nose broke the surface of the water, the horn shrilled. It shrilled the most feared call of all. It was the fateful sound of RECALL. Only some horses galloped back. Only some horses' lips never touched the water. Only those were the horses that passed the final test. Only those were the horses that were kept. Only those would be entrusted with the lives of the fearless Bedouin.

Main Idea   1

	Answer	Score
Mark the *main idea*	M	15
Mark the statement that is *too broad*	B	5
Mark the statement that is *too narrow*	N	5

a. The armies of Arabia used horses for combat and camels for patrol. ☐ _____

b. Arabian horses were bred through difficult tests and training. ☐ _____

c. The horse was important to the armies of Arabia. ☐ _____

Subject Matter

2 This passage is mostly about
☐ a. Arabian combat.
☐ b. why Arabs bred horses.
☐ c. training Arabian horses.
☐ d. armies of Arabia. _____

Supporting
Details

3 During the final test the horses
☐ a. could not drink anything.
☐ b. heard the horn constantly.
☐ c. could only drink lake water.
☐ d. were fed hay. _____

Conclusion

4 We can conclude from this passage that
☐ a. Arabian trainers also fought in the army.
☐ b. the horses that passed the test fought in battle.
☐ c. the horses that did not pass were used for
patrol duty.
☐ d. camels also had to survive tests and training. _____

Clarifying
Devices

5 The author makes the horse training process
clearer to the reader by
☐ a. describing a particular training activity.
☐ b. presenting a well-planned argument.
☐ c. narrating some eyewitness accounts.
☐ d. telling a story about a successful horse. _____

Vocabulary
in Context

6 Tumult, in this passage, means
☐ a. excitement.
☐ b. commotion.
☐ c. killing.
☐ d. fear. _____

**Add your scores for questions 1–6. Enter the total here
and on the graph on page 214.** Total
Score _____

83 The Long and Short of It

Every day we lace our talk with measurement words. We ask, "How much?" "How many?" and "How far?" At the store we buy meat by the pound, clothing by the size, and cloth by the yard. All athletic events are played on measured fields or surfaces. Rules are also filled with words of measurement. For example, in football we know that a first down means a gain of at least 10 yards. Words of distance, weight, and size help us understand and visualize what is seen or said.

In ancient times, people used parts of the body as units of measurement. The Romans used *uncia* to name the distance equal to the width of a thumb. The English picked up this word and renamed it an *inch*. They did not, however, accept the thumb as a unit of measure. They decided instead that an inch should be "three barley corns, round and dry, placed end-to-end lengthwise."

After this inch was accepted and used, the English then joined 12 inches and called it a *foot*. As it happened, 12 inches was roughly the length of a man's foot, so the foot-unit was widely used. To measure a room, all you had to do was put one foot in front of the other and count.

The inch and the foot worked so well that the English introduced a larger unit. They put together three lengths of a man's foot and called it a *yard*. Again, man had another useful unit—in this case, one he could use to pace off a large field quickly.

Then the English made a unit for the women, one especially for measuring cloth. They called this unit a *yard* too. The distance was from a man's nose to the tip of his middle finger.

Of course, there is a <u>flaw</u> in all this. Not all men are the same size. But no one seems to care.

Main Idea	1		
		Answer	**Score**
	Mark the *main idea*	**M**	**15**
	Mark the statement that is *too broad*	**B**	**5**
	Mark the statement that is *too narrow*	**N**	**5**

a. The problems of measurement began centuries ago. ☐ _____

b. The English recognized the need for a standard inch. ☐ _____

c. Various units of measurement developed over the centuries. ☐ _____

Subject Matter   **2**   This article is mainly concerned with
- ☐ a. Roman measurement.
- ☐ b. the development of common units of measurement.
- ☐ c. what an inch and a foot are equal to.
- ☐ d. understanding measurement.   _____

Supporting Details   **3**   The Romans decided that
- ☐ a. thumbs were about an inch wide.
- ☐ b. barleycorns were always the same size.
- ☐ c. people are not all the same size.
- ☐ d. a man's foot measures exactly 12 inches.   _____

Conclusion   **4**   Many units of measurement were developed
- ☐ a. to make it easier to figure out common lengths.
- ☐ b. because men were considered more important than women.
- ☐ c. for no particular reason.
- ☐ d. so the English could prove their superiority to the Romans.   _____

Clarifying Devices   **5**   In the first paragraph the author gives
- ☐ a. a history of measurement.
- ☐ b. examples of how often we use measures.
- ☐ c. an explanation of football rules.
- ☐ d. a way of figuring out which measures are useful.   _____

Vocabulary in Context   **6**   The word <u>flaw</u> is closest in meaning to
- ☐ a. defect.
- ☐ b. difference.
- ☐ c. change.
- ☐ d. danger.   _____

Add your scores for questions 1–6. Enter the total here and on the graph on page 214.   **Total Score**   _____

84 The Royal Canadian Mounted Police

What group was named the NorthWest Mounted Rifles? Back in 1873, this was the first name given to the Canadian Mounted Police. Why did the original name change? Because the United States objected. They thought the name sounded too much like a military force. And that was a problem. A treaty between the United States and Canada stated that no armed forces would patrol the 4,000-mile border. So the name became Canadian Mounted Police. The word *royal* was added in 1920. King Edward VII of England allowed them to use the prefix.

What is the mission of the Mounties? The words on their badge tell it all. The words are "Maintain the right." The Mounties cover miles and miles of territory to fulfill their mission. They are not like the local police in towns and cities. Their territory is the mountains, forests, and tundra of the rest of Canada.

The Mounties gained world fame during the Klondike gold rush. Gold was discovered in August 1896. More than 25,000 people joined the rush. People from all over the world sought their <u>fortune</u> in the frozen north. The Mounties kept law and order in the Canadian gold fields. (Many people believe the gold rush took place in Alaska. This is not so. The gold rush was in the Yukon Territory. This belongs to Canada.)

In ceremonies, you can still see the Mounties. You'll see the famous scarlet tunics that they wear. You'll also see their wide-brimmed hats. Their breeches are always tucked in high boots with spurs. Dressed to the hilt, the Mounties are a sight to see.

Main Idea	1	Answer	Score
	Mark the *main idea*	M	15
	Mark the statement that is *too broad*	B	5
	Mark the statement that is *too narrow*	N	5

a. The Royal Mounties are Canadian law officers. ☐ ____

b. The Mounties became famous during the gold rush. ☐ ____

c. The Royal Mounties have policed Canadian territory for over a hundred years. ☐ ____

Subject Matter **2** This passage is mainly about
☐ a. the treaty between U.S. and Canada.
☐ b. Canadian police.
☐ c. the Royal Mounties.
☐ d. a Canadian mission.

_____

Supporting Details **3** The Royal Mounties are recognized by their
☐ a. white shirts.
☐ b. highly polished shoes.
☐ c. short, dark hats.
☐ d. scarlet tunics.

_____

Conclusion **4** The Mounties became famous during the Klondike gold rush because
☐ a. they kept order and control over thousands of people.
☐ b. it was cold and crowded but they stayed in the gold fields.
☐ c. they helped discover the gold territory.
☐ d. more people came to see the Mounties than ever before.

_____

Clarifying Devices **5** To explain how the Mounties got their present name, the author
☐ a. tells a detailed story about Edward VII of England.
☐ b. describes their uniforms.
☐ c. compares them to other policing forces.
☐ d. refers to a U.S.-Canadian treaty.

_____

Vocabulary in Context **6** As used in this passage, <u>fortune</u> means
☐ a. luck.
☐ b. future.
☐ c. wealth.
☐ d. goods.

_____

Add your scores for questions 1–6. Enter the total here and on the graph on page 214. **Total Score**

_____

85 Protecting the Orange Crop

Frost on the windowpanes is a child's dream. Frost in the orange groves is a grower's nightmare. Here is the reason: frost can ruin the oranges and even kill the trees. How does this happen? When the temperature is below 32 degrees Fahrenheit, juices in the leaves and oranges freeze. When it freezes, the juice expands. This swelling bursts the thin cells of the leaves and fruit. Then the oranges will spoil and the trees dry up.

When growers hear a forecast of frost, they act fast. Smudge pots ready for lighting are placed in the groves. Oil burners are also put out. Both are costly. For example, to protect an orange grove, 20 to 100 heaters are needed per acre.

Smudge pots and heaters are two ways of fighting frost. But now there is a new way. Odd as it sounds, growers use ice to fight freezing! Some spray their crops with water on a freezing night. The water freezes quickly, and then a strange thing happens. As long as ice stays wet, it can't get colder than 32 degrees. Trees and oranges can stand this temperature. If the ice ever became entirely frozen and dry, it might drop many degrees and ruin the crop. The trick is to continually spray water on the ice. The spraying keeps the temperature from going below 32 degrees even if the air is much colder. Jack Frost may be <u>frustrated</u>, but the oranges and trees are saved.

This strange kind of "ice blanket" works only on plants strong enough to stand the weight of frozen spray. The system is also used to protect banana plants on some Central American plantations.

Main Idea 1

	Answer	Score
Mark the *main idea*	M	15
Mark the statement that is *too broad*	B	5
Mark the statement that is *too narrow*	N	5

a. Oranges and orange trees can withstand ice. ☐ _____

b. Frost can be prevented from killing plants. ☐ _____

c. Orange trees can be protected from freezing in several ways. ☐ _____

Subject Matter   2   The best alternate title for this passage is
    ☐ a. Jack Frost Triumphs Again.
    ☐ b. Ways to Battle Frost.
    ☐ c. The Helpless Plant.
    ☐ d. The Battle of the Farmer.   _____

Supporting Details   3   Ice can save fruit trees rather than destroy them if the trees are
    ☐ a. strong enough to support it.
    ☐ b. sprayed periodically.
    ☐ c. accustomed to frost.
    ☐ d. quickly defrosted.   _____

Conclusion   4   You can conclude from the passage that ice would not be used to prevent the freezing of
    ☐ a. banana trees.
    ☐ b. fir trees.
    ☐ c. delicate rose bushes.
    ☐ d. apple orchards.   _____

Clarifying Devices   5   The first paragraph catches the reader's attention with
    ☐ a. vivid adjectives.
    ☐ b. an interesting comparison.
    ☐ c. personal opinions.
    ☐ d. a definition.   _____

Vocabulary in Context   6   As used in this passage, <u>frustrated</u> means
    ☐ a. pleased.
    ☐ b. irritated.
    ☐ c. melted.
    ☐ d. said no to.   _____

Add your scores for questions 1–6. Enter the total here and on the graph on page 214.   **Total Score**   _____

86 Nighttime Sleep

Here is a statistic that will surprise you. More young people are killed each year by sleepy drivers than by drunk drivers. This proves one thing. Getting enough sleep can be a big problem. How are we dealing with the problem? Sleep clinics are popping up all over the United States. They are always working to find out more about sleep.

Driving when tired can be very dangerous. During the daytime, over half of drivers report feeling sleepy at some point. At night, over 80 percent of drivers sometimes get drowsy. And here is the most frightening of all. Almost one-quarter of all drivers have fallen asleep at the wheel.

What is going on here? One thing is that people are not getting enough sleep. One person out of three gets by on less than six hours a night. Many people have trouble falling asleep. Others fall asleep easily, but then wake up time after time. Few people get enough of the deep sleep they need to feel really rested.

Here are some facts to remember. Believe it or not, people need seven to nine hours of nighttime sleep to remain healthy. During that sleep, a person's immune system is built up. This helps fight off diseases and infections. And taking a nap in the daytime does not really help. It will make a person feel <u>refreshed</u>. But it cannot make up for the lack of nighttime sleep.

What if you are a person with real sleeping problems? What if you have tried all the home remedies like hot milk? You might consider going to a sleep clinic. Many such clinics look for volunteers. They will study your sleep problems, and you will not have to pay anything.

Main Idea	1	Answer	Score
	Mark the *main idea*	M	15
	Mark the statement that is *too broad*	B	5
	Mark the statement that is *too narrow*	N	5

a. Nighttime sleep is important in preventing illness and unsafe driving. ☐ _____

b. Sleepy drivers can cause accidents and kill people. ☐ _____

c. Getting proper sleep is necessary for everyone. ☐ _____

Score 15 points for each correct answer.　　**Score**

Subject Matter　**2**　This passage is mainly concerned with
　　　☐ a. sleepy drivers.
　　　☐ b. data about sleep and sleepers.
　　　☐ c. taking naps.
　　　☐ d. sleep clinics.　　　　_____

Supporting
Details　**3**　Proper sleep
　　　☐ a. can be had either at night or during the day.
　　　☐ b. is about 10 hours a night.
　　　☐ c. strengthens the immune system.
　　　☐ d. is less necessary as people get older.　　　_____

Conclusion　**4**　We can assume that lack of sleep could
　　　☐ a. make a person gain weight.
　　　☐ b. not happen at a sleep clinic.
　　　☐ c. be dangerous for pilots.
　　　☐ d. have a bad effect on animals.　　　_____

Clarifying
Devices　**5**　To help the reader understand that sleep is
　　　important, the writer uses
　　　☐ a. several examples.
　　　☐ b. quotes from experts.
　　　☐ c. careful measurements.
　　　☐ d. strong arguments.　　　_____

Vocabulary
in Context　**6**　The best definition for <u>refreshed</u> in this passage is
　　　☐ a. newly purchased.
　　　☐ b. restored.
　　　☐ c. newly planted.
　　　☐ d. quiet.　　　_____

**Add your scores for questions 1–6. Enter the total here
and on the graph on page 214.**　　**Total
Score**　_____

87 The *Titanic*

The word "unsinkable" sunk the *Titanic*. How? Because everyone believed it.

The ship left Southampton, England, on April 10, 1912. She sailed for five days on calm seas, steaming at about 26 miles per hour. Pretty fast for a ship of over 46 thousand tons.

On April 14, wireless re0ports from other ships warned of icebergs ahead. Actually, six reports came in that day. But the "unsinkable" ship steamed on. No slowing down.

There was no moon that night. At 11:40 P.M. lookout Frederick Fleet saw the iceberg and phoned the bridge. A mountain of ice loomed against the dark sky. The berg was about 100 feet high. This means it extended about 900 feet below the surface. The ship <u>veered</u> at the last second. From above, it looked like a close shave. But at the bottom a scraping sound was heard.

It took 25 minutes to assess the damage. Water was pouring in. At 12:05, "Get the lifeboats ready" was ordered. By 2:20 A.M. the ship had sunk below the surface. So there were only about two free hours to load the lifeboats. The ship carried 2,207 people. Fully loaded, the lifeboats could take only 1,178. Already there was guaranteed doom for many. Most boats pulled away partially loaded. Boat #1, made for 40, carried only 12. Ultimately, only 705 people survived.

Just 10 miles away was the *Californian*, stopped since 10:30 P.M. Each ship could see the other's lights. But they could not communicate. The *Californian* shut down its wireless at 11:30. The *Titanic* crashed 10 minutes later. Its cry for help was unheard.

The *Carpathia*, many miles away, heard. Arriving after four hours, it picked up the survivors.

Main Idea   1

	Answer	Score
Mark the *main idea*	M	15
Mark the statement that is *too broad*	B	5
Mark the statement that is *too narrow*	N	5

a. There is really no such thing as an unsinkable ship. ☐ ____

b. The sinking of the *Titanic* is an unforgettably sad and tragic story. ☐ ____

c. A huge iceberg struck the bottom of the *Titanic*. ☐ ____

Score 15 points for each correct answer.

Subject Matter   **2**   Another good title for this passage would be
- [ ] a. "Man the Lifeboats!"
- [ ] b. Just One Small Iceberg.
- [ ] c. A Beautiful Ocean Liner.
- [ ] d. A Watery Disaster.

_____

Supporting Details   **3**   When the *Titanic* hit the iceberg it
- [ ] a. wired the *Californian.*
- [ ] b. had lifeboats ready.
- [ ] c. was night.
- [ ] d. immediately notified the passengers.

_____

Conclusion   **4**   From this passage we can infer that
- [ ] a. the *Titanic* did not have a large enough crew.
- [ ] b. passengers were not told to fill the lifeboats.
- [ ] c. more woman and children survived.
- [ ] d. most ships did not care what happened to others.

_____

Clarifying Devices   **5**   The first paragraph in the passage suggests that
- [ ] a. no one was properly prepared for an emergency on the ship.
- [ ] b. if the ship was built correctly it would not have sunk.
- [ ] c. there should have been lifeboat drills on the ship.
- [ ] d. the *Titanic* was destined to sink.

_____

Vocabulary in Context   **6**   As used in this passage, <u>veered</u> means
- [ ] a. steered.
- [ ] b. swerved.
- [ ] c. backed up.
- [ ] d. rocked.

_____

Add your scores for questions 1–6. Enter the total here and on the graph on page 214.   **Total Score**   _____

88 The Panama Canal

Here are some basics about the Panama Canal. It cuts through Panama to join the Atlantic and Pacific oceans. Work on it started in 1904. The first ship sailed through on August 15, 1914. The canal is 50.72 miles long. From ocean to ocean, travel time is about eight hours.

What makes the canal so important is this. Ships don't have to sail around the tip of South America. For example, consider a ship sailing from New York City to San Francisco. Sailing around South America is 13,000 miles. Going through the canal is about 5,200 miles less.

About 40 ships pass through the canal in a day. All ships, including warships, must pay a toll. The toll depends on a ship's size and cargo. For example, the U.S.S. *New Jersey* paid $28,838. The German ship *Hamburg* paid $40,936. Warships are allowed to use the canal, but only in peacetime.

What was the greatest problem in building the canal? The answer: disease. The Canal Zone was one of the most disease-ridden areas in the world. In 1904, Colonel William Gorgas was put in charge of improving health conditions. He was a doctor. He had already gained fame by wiping out yellow fever in Cuba. His first two years were devoted to sanitation. Swamps were drained. Brush was cleared. Tall and short grasses were cut. By 1906, Gorgas had wiped out yellow fever. He eliminated the rats that carried bubonic plague. He did not completely wipe out malaria. But he greatly <u>reduced</u> its rate. So it is fair to say this. The canal engineers were great. But the project would never have been completed without William Gorgas.

Main Idea	1		
		Answer	**Score**
Mark the *main idea*		M	15
Mark the statement that is *too broad*		B	5
Mark the statement that is *too narrow*		N	5

a. The Panama Canal was an important development in the 1900s. ☐ _____

b. Ships pay a toll to pass through the Panama Canal. ☐ _____

c. The Panama Canal saves travel time, but it was not built without a struggle. ☐ _____

Subject Matter   **2**   The passage is primarily about
    ☐ a. sailing through the canal.
    ☐ b. Colonel William Gorgas.
    ☐ c. the Panama Canal.
    ☐ d. what people did before the canal was built.   _____

Supporting Details   **3**   The Panama Canal
    ☐ a. has about 40 ships sailing through in a day.
    ☐ b. does not charge a toll to American ships.
    ☐ c. was completed in 1904.
    ☐ d. goes from New York City to San Francisco.   _____

Conclusion   **4**   Judging from this passage, one might say that building the canal
    ☐ a. caused diseases that hurt people in the area.
    ☐ b. made it easier for warships to fight other countries.
    ☐ c. made sailing more expensive than it had been.
    ☐ d. took courage and dedication.   _____

Clarifying Devices   **5**   The author makes clear how difficult canal building was by
    ☐ a. describing the work of Gorgas.
    ☐ b. describing the tall mountains that surround it.
    ☐ c. giving the number of people who died building it.
    ☐ d. telling how long it took to build.   _____

Vocabulary in Context   **6**   In this passage reduced means
    ☐ a. decreased.
    ☐ b. improved.
    ☐ c. measured.
    ☐ d. enlarged.   _____

Add your scores for questions 1–6. Enter the total here and on the graph on page 214.   Total Score   _____

89 Knives, Forks, and Spoons

Imagine sitting down to dinner in the early days of our country. In front of you at that time would be a large plate made of pewter. Alongside the pewter plate would be only a knife and a spoon. What? No fork? Yes, no fork. Why? The first fork was brought to this country by Governor John Winthrop in 1630. It took many years before the average family had forks.

Even when forks were introduced, they were not widely used. They were thought to be effeminate. This was true especially among men. Tough men continued to pick up food with their fingers. Even the clergy jumped to the side of such men. They argued that it was almost a sin to eat with a fork. After all, they said, fingers were made before forks. Also, forks were an unnatural substitute for the God-given fingers.

Nevertheless, forks slowly gained acceptance. The earliest ones had only two tines. The tines were not delicate. They were long and looked more like a weapon than an eating utensil. For a better idea of what they looked like, do this. Open your kitchen drawer and take out the fork used in carving a big turkey or roast beef. This is a <u>throwback</u> to the early table forks. And these carving forks, in turn, were a throwback to a vicious twin-pointed battle spear.

The forks we now use have either three or four tines. Such forks came into use only about a century ago. You may wonder how such a simple utensil took so long to develop. After all, hundreds of complex inventions came about long before the fork. Why didn't people's ingenuity come to the fore a lot sooner? We don't know. What's your guess?

Main Idea	1		
		Answer	Score
Mark the *main idea*		M	15
Mark the statement that is *too broad*		B	5
Mark the statement that is *too narrow*		N	5
a. The fork's development took many years.		☐	_____
b. Utensils take years to be accepted.		☐	_____
c. The early fork was similar to a carving fork.		☐	_____

Subject Matter **2** The focus of this passage is
    ☐ a. utensils.
    ☐ b. the early days.
    ☐ c. the development of the fork.
    ☐ d. simple inventions.   _____

Supporting Details **3** Early forks
    ☐ a. were sometimes used as battle spears.
    ☐ b. were more useful than modern forks.
    ☐ c. were used only for carving.
    ☐ d. originally had only two tines.   _____

Conclusion **4** From this passage we can conclude that today's forks
    ☐ a. are used more widely than when forks were first developed.
    ☐ b. come in many sizes.
    ☐ c. are enjoying renewed popularity.
    ☐ d. are closely related to spoons.   _____

Clarifying Devices **5** The purpose of the first sentence in this passage is to
    ☐ a. jog your memory.
    ☐ b. help you visualize.
    ☐ c. put you in a serious mood.
    ☐ d. awaken your feelings.   _____

Vocabulary in Context **6** The word <u>throwback</u>, as used in this passage, means
    ☐ a. an object that is able to return to the sender.
    ☐ b. something that bounces back.
    ☐ c. an object related to a similar, earlier object.
    ☐ d. a valuable object.   _____

Add your scores for questions 1–6. Enter the total here and on the graph on page 214.   Total Score   _____

90 A Seed Takes a Bow

You probably remember that chocolate is made from cacao seeds. These seeds grow on cacao trees. Note that *cacao* (not cocoa) is the <u>accurate</u> spelling. The mistake in spelling was made a long time ago by English importers.

The word *cacao* comes from two Mayan words meaning "bitter juice." The word *chocolate* came from two other Mayan words meaning "warm drink."

The cacao tree was first found in southern Mexico. In their wild state cacao trees grow up to 40 feet tall. But on a farm they are kept pruned to a height of about 15 feet.

Cacao trees require a mean temperature of about 80 degrees. They just cannot stand a cold or even cool climate. Another requirement is that they cannot stand direct sunlight. They are sensitive when young. They grow best in the shade of other trees. For example, they seem to like such trees as mango, rubber, banana, or breadfruit.

The cacao seed grows in a pod that looks like a long cucumber. It can be 14 inches long. Pods do not hang on stems. They pop directly out of a bare trunk or cling to the bare branches.

When the pods are ripe they are cut open. Each pod contains 25 to 50 seeds or beans. On the average, they are about an inch wide. The seeds are then taken out and fermented. When cured, no pulp clings to the seed. The yield, on the average, is one to two pounds of seed per tree per year. So you need many trees to satisfy the market. Most of the world's cacao comes from small family farms. The biggest producers are Ghana in West Africa and Brazil in South America.

Main Idea	1		
		Answer	**Score**
	Mark the *main idea*	**M**	**15**
	Mark the statement that is *too broad*	**B**	**5**
	Mark the statement that is *too narrow*	**N**	**5**
	a. The cacao seed grows in a long pod.	☐	____
	b. Cacao seeds and trees have distinct characteristics.	☐	____
	c. Cacao trees produce cacao seeds.	☐	____

Score 15 points for each correct answer.   **Score**

Subject Matter   **2** This passage deals mainly with
- [ ] a. where cacao trees are grown.
- [ ] b. cacao seeds and cacao trees.
- [ ] c. cacao trees.
- [ ] d. products made from cacao seeds.   _____

Supporting   **3** The cacao tree was first discovered in
Details
- [ ] a. Ghana.
- [ ] b. southern Mexico.
- [ ] c. Brazil.
- [ ] d. the southern United States.   _____

Conclusion   **4** It is possible to conclude that the cacao tree
- [ ] a. makes more pods if it is in the shade.
- [ ] b. is more popular in Mexico than anywhere else.
- [ ] c. grows under another tree because it likes company.
- [ ] d. is a fairly fussy plant.   _____

Clarifying   **5** When referring to the "mean" temperature, the
Devices   author is referring to the
- [ ] a. temperature that trees are forced to grow in.
- [ ] b. temperature colder than the trees would like.
- [ ] c. exact temperature necessary for cacao trees to live.
- [ ] d. average temperature suitable for cacao trees to grow.   _____

Vocabulary   **6** As used in this passage, <u>accurate</u> means
in Context
- [ ] a. incorrect.
- [ ] b. correct.
- [ ] c. old.
- [ ] d. about the same.   _____

**Add your scores for questions 1–6. Enter the total here   Total
and on the graph on page 214.   Score**   _____

91 Icebergs

Fog at sea is dangerous. But icebergs at sea are terrifying. Just the mention of icebergs and we immediately think *Titanic.* Even though that ship struck a large berg, we know icebergs can be even larger. One of the largest ever seen was in the Antarctic region. It was 60 miles wide. It was over 200 miles long. Let us compare it to one of our states. It was twice as big as the state of Connecticut. An even more important measure of size is the depth of an iceberg. For example, the Antarctic berg <u>towered</u> about 400 feet above the surface of the ocean. But this was only about an eighth to a tenth of its total mass. Most of the berg—3,600 feet in this case—was under water.

How are icebergs formed? The iceberg first of all was part of a glacier or ice cap on land. The thickest ice cap of all is the Antarctic ice cap. It is 1,000 feet thick near the coast and 6,000 feet thick in the middle. The 6,000 foot portion is heavy beyond imagination. This weight in the middle puts pressure on the whole ice cap. The pressure pushes out the ice at the ends. The ends are pushed into the sea. When these ends break off, they become floating icebergs.

Let's shift to the North Atlantic. The bergs here break off the ice cap covering Greenland. The danger is that some of these bergs float into the routes of transatlantic liners. April, May, and June are the worst months. During these months, ships take a more southerly route.

Ships traveling at night are in special danger. After the *Titanic,* an ice patrol was formed to protect all ships. Ice patrols use planes and ships to locate icebergs. The patrol reports the position of all icebergs. It also charts the bergs' probable courses. No one wants another *Titanic!*

Main Idea	1		
		Answer	**Score**
	Mark the *main idea*	M	15
	Mark the statement that is *too broad*	B	5
	Mark the statement that is *too narrow*	N	5
	a. Icebergs are formed from ice caps and glaciers.	☐	_____
	b. There are many dangers for ships in ice-filled waters.	☐	_____
	c. Icebergs' size and weight make them dangerous for ships.	☐	_____

Score 15 points for each correct answer. Score

Subject Matter 2 This passage is mainly about
☐ a. the *Titanic*.
☐ b. icebergs from Antarctica.
☐ c. dangers from icebergs.
☐ d. what ice caps are.   _____

Supporting 3 One of the largest known icebergs came from
Details
☐ a. Greenland.
☐ b. the Arctic Circle.
☐ c. Antarctica.
☐ d. Iceland.   _____

Conclusion 4 If a ship were to travel from New York to England
in April, it would probably
☐ a. use the northerly route.
☐ b. use the southerly route.
☐ c. travel only in daytime.
☐ d. consider postponing until May.   _____

Clarifying 5 To describe the length of the largest iceberg the
Devices   author uses
☐ a. true accounts.
☐ b. humor.
☐ c. a story.
☐ d. a comparison.   _____

Vocabulary 6 In this passage, the word <u>towered</u> is closest in
in Context   meaning to
☐ a. reached.
☐ b. extended in height.
☐ c. extended in width.
☐ d. bent.   _____

Add your scores for questions 1–6. Enter the total here   Total
and on the graph on page 214.   Score   _____

92 Indispensable Rubber

Pearl Harbor. It was December 7, 1941. Japanese bombers destroyed or damaged 19 American ships. The loss was a nightmare. Nothing could be worse. But a greater loss came right after that. What happened was that there was no rubber.

The Japanese had captured almost all the rubber-growing lands. These were lands in the Far East. Nine-tenths of the world's supply of natural rubber was no longer available.

Without rubber, war production would stop. There was no doubt about it. Everything needed rubber. Trucks, jeeps, and planes needed tires. Artillery could not move. Shipbuilding would cease. The Army and Navy could not move. Rubber was a must. To emphasize: this was a greater crisis than Pearl Harbor.

What did the United States do? Latex, the sap from a rubber tree, was needed. But goldenrod and dandelions also produce latex. Fields of both were planted. Some latex was produced, but only small amounts. Desperation set in. Much more was needed. And quickly.

There was only one sure answer, to produce <u>synthetic</u> rubber. Chemists worked around the clock. They were successful. A fine rubber was quickly produced from oil. Production of war materials never stopped. American soldiers could be supplied.

After the war, new plantations were planted. Some were in South America, some in West Africa. Botanists developed better trees. These produce six times more latex than wild trees. Even hormones and vitamins are used to increase yields. The U.S. does not want to be caught short.

Main Idea   1

	Answer	Score
Mark the *main idea*	M	15
Mark the statement that is *too broad*	B	5
Mark the statement that is *too narrow*	N	5

a. The loss of rubber was greater than the loss of ships in Pearl Harbor. ☐ _____

b. Wartime shortages can cause great hardships. ☐ _____

c. After Pearl Harbor, the U.S. searched desperately for new sources for rubber. ☐ _____

Subject Matter   **2**   The passage centers on

☐ a. finding an alternative rubber supply.

☐ b. making rubber.

☐ c. military problems after Pearl Harbor.

☐ d. production of rubber in the U.S.   _____

Supporting Details   **3**   Rubber was needed for

☐ a. children's toys.

☐ b. truck tires.

☐ c. tires for people's cars.

☐ d. soldiers' uniforms.   _____

Conclusion   **4**   From the last sentence you can guess that the U.S.

☐ a. will not go to war again.

☐ b. buys up large rubber plantations during wars.

☐ c. will have a method for supplying rubber in the future.

☐ d. has increased its production of rubber.   _____

Clarifying Devices   **5**   Pearl Harbor is described in the first paragraph to

☐ a. explain the hardships of war.

☐ b. show what a beautiful, peaceful place it had been.

☐ c. give the reader a historical time frame.

☐ d. remind the reader how terrible and destructive war can be.   _____

Vocabulary in Context   **6**   If something is <u>synthetic</u> it is

☐ a. made of rubber.

☐ b. created from plants.

☐ c. man-made.

☐ d. natural.   _____

Add your scores for questions 1–6. Enter the total here and on the graph on page 214.   **Total Score**   _____

93 Gold and a Stagecoach Hero

Somehow the word *gold*, even in a hushed whisper, does strange things to people. What do people do? They rush, almost in a panic, to the newly discovered fields. For example, over 10,000 rushed to Alaska to pan the Klondike gold.

But one of the biggest rushes was to California in the 1840s. The "forty-niners" poured in from all parts of the world to pan the rich deposits. The miners brought thousands of ounces of gold into the banks. This was a good business for the banks, but it also presented a problem. The gold had to be moved eastward to stronger banks. The only transportation was the stagecoach.

Bandits, of course, would watch for shipments of gold. Watching paid off. A man named Sam Bass, for instance, stole $50,000 in gold. A fortune in those early days!

The favorite target of bandits was the stagecoach. The bandits would pick a deserted spot. In such a spot some bandits <u>waylaid</u> Charley Parkhurst's stagecoach. Parkhurst was a stagecoach driver widely known for driving skill. The first time he was stopped and threatened, he gave up the gold. But he said, "I wasn't expecting this, but the next time, I'll be ready for you."

The next time came soon. And, as promised, Charley was ready. He shot the leader of the ill-starred gang. Then he whipped his horses right through the gang. They scattered like rabbits.

What made Charley's feat all the more remarkable was revealed at his death in 1879. The doctor's death certificate showed that Charley, old rough-and-tumble Charley, was actually *Charlotte* Parkhurst.

Main Idea	1		
		Answer	**Score**
Mark the *main idea*		M	15
Mark the statement that is *too broad*		B	5
Mark the statement that is *too narrow*		N	5

a. Charley Parkhurst's stagecoach was held up. ☐ _____

b. Gold rushes presented problems. ☐ _____

c. Gold bandits targeted stagecoaches but were outsmarted by Charley Parkhurst. ☐ _____

Score 15 points for each correct answer. **Score**

Subject Matter   **2**   The main subject of this passage is
- ☐ a. the dangers of the stagecoach.
- ☐ b. the life of Charley Parkhurst.
- ☐ c. the death of Charley Parkhurst.
- ☐ d. transporting gold.

_____

Supporting Details   **3**   The bandits were looking for
- ☐ a. stagecoaches.
- ☐ b. gold rushes.
- ☐ c. bank officials.
- ☐ d. shipments of gold.

_____

Conclusion   **4**   The passage suggests that a stagecoach driver was assumed to be
- ☐ a. a man.
- ☐ b. frightened of bandits.
- ☐ c. sympathetic to bandits.
- ☐ d. young and good looking.

_____

Clarifying Devices   **5**   The adjective "ill-starred" describes the gang's
- ☐ a. intentions.
- ☐ b. reputation.
- ☐ c. luck.
- ☐ d. skill.

_____

Vocabulary in Context   **6**   As used in this passage, <u>waylaid</u> most closely means
- ☐ a. attacked and captured.
- ☐ b. chased and destroyed.
- ☐ c. attacked from a hiding place and robbed.
- ☐ d. forced to turn around and go back.

_____

Add your scores for questions 1–6. Enter the total here and on the graph on page 214.

Total Score _____

94 Diners

Do you know what a diner is? These days it is a restaurant with booths and a long counter. Diners have a long history in America. But they used to look quite different.

The first diners appeared in 1872. This was in Rhode Island. A Mr. Walter Scott had the first horsedrawn diner. He sat on a box in the back of a covered wagon. Inside the wagon were chicken sandwiches. Scott would drive up to a factory. He would sell night workers sandwiches. He passed them through a hole in the covered wagon.

The first <u>stationary</u> diner appeared 15 years later. It was a walk-in place in Massachusetts, with stools and a kitchen. Sandwiches, deserts, coffee, and milk were available.

Diners began to look very interesting in the 1900s. Most of the horsedrawn ones were now standing along the sides of roads. But they kept their wagon shapes. Then unused trolley cars began to be converted to diners. The long, thin shape of these cars was perfect for a counter and some stools. As trains became very stream-lined, many diners began to look like fancy train cars. They took on a sleek, smooth, silver appearance. Their insides were made of stainless steel and Formica. By the end of the 1930s, they usually had flashing neon signs outside. Perhaps you have seen diners like these in old movies.

For a while, it seemed that the classic diner was making a comeback. Many old ones were restored. Fancy ones were built new in a few big cities. The food in a diner is never extraordinary. Usually it is hamburgers or meat loaf. But people love these places for their atmosphere.

Main Idea	1			
			Answer	**Score**
	Mark the _main idea_		M	15
	Mark the statement that is _too broad_		B	5
	Mark the statement that is _too narrow_		N	5
	a. Most restaurants change over time.		☐	____
	b. Some diners were restored trolley cars.		☐	____
	c. Diners gradually changed from simple to rather classy eating places.		☐	____

Score 15 points for each correct answer.   Score

Subject Matter   **2**   Another good title for this passage would be
    ☐ a. Building a Diner.
    ☐ b. Dining in Style.
    ☐ c. The Horsedrawn Diner.
    ☐ d. Dining on Hamburgers and Meat Loaf.   _____

Supporting   **3**   The first diner appeared in
Details
    ☐ a. the 1930s.
    ☐ b. 1900.
    ☐ c. 1887.
    ☐ d. 1872.   _____

Conclusion   **4**   In the 1930s, the best diners looked rather
    ☐ a. large.
    ☐ b. square-shaped.
    ☐ c. brightly colored.
    ☐ d. stylish.   _____

Clarifying   **5**   The author presents the discussion of diners in
Devices
    ☐ a. spatial order.
    ☐ b. order of importance.
    ☐ c. order of difficulty.
    ☐ d. chronological order.   _____

Vocabulary   **6**   In this passage <u>stationary</u> means
in Context
    ☐ a. not moving.
    ☐ b. something to write on.
    ☐ c. made of bricks.
    ☐ d. made of paper.   _____

Add your scores for questions 1–6. Enter the total here   Total
and on the graph on page 214.   Score   _____

95 Remarkable Lakes

North America has some pretty unique lakes. For example, five of the world's largest lakes are here. They are the Great Lakes. Put them together. They form the world's biggest body of fresh water.

Superior is the largest Great Lake. It is also the biggest freshwater lake in the world. Superior's area is almost 32,000 square miles. At its deepest point this huge lake is over 1,300 feet deep. Superior is on the border between Northern Michigan and Ontario. Its water never gets very warm. This is because it is so far north. Even in summer, it may be only 45 to 50 degrees.

The next Great Lake is Huron. It is about 200 miles long. It covers about 23,000 square miles. Like Superior, it <u>straddles</u> the United States-Canadian border. Also like Superior, few cities of any size dot its banks.

Lake Huron is directly connected to Lake Michigan. This is the third Great Lake. It is the only one completely inside the United States. It is farther south than the other two. So its waters warm up a bit in the summer. For example, near its southern tip it may reach over 70 degrees. Chicago and Milwaukee are two big cities on Lake Michigan.

The final Great Lakes are Ontario and Erie. These lakes are quite a bit smaller than the others. Lake Erie borders on three states and Ontario. Lake Ontario borders on only one state. These two lakes lie close to each other. They have many cities built along them. These include Cleveland, Buffalo, and Toronto. One difference between them is this. Lake Erie is very shallow. But parts of Lake Ontario are very deep. At one point this lake is 800 feet deep.

Main Idea	1	Answer	Score
	Mark the *main idea*	M	15
	Mark the statement that is *too broad*	B	5
	Mark the statement that is *too narrow*	N	5

a. Chicago and Toronto are located on the Great Lakes. ☐ _____

b. There are five Great Lakes. ☐ _____

c. The Great Lakes have distinct characteristics. ☐ _____

Score 15 points for each correct answer.   **Score**

Subject Matter   **2**   This passage deals mainly with
- [ ] a. physical characteristics of the Great Lakes.
- [ ] b. large lakes in the world.
- [ ] c. Lake Superior.
- [ ] d. shipping on the Great Lakes.   _____

Supporting Details   **3**   The only Great Lake completely inside the United States is
- [ ] a. Erie.
- [ ] b. Superior.
- [ ] c. Huron.
- [ ] d. Michigan.   _____

Conclusion   **4**   It is safe to conclude from the article that
- [ ] a. cities are more likely to be built along the warmer lakes.
- [ ] b. Lake Superior has many resorts for swimming.
- [ ] c. Lake Michigan was discovered first.
- [ ] d. the five lakes are not that close together.   _____

Clarifying Devices   **5**   The author develops this passage mainly by
- [ ] a. telling stories.
- [ ] b. pointing out similarities and differences.
- [ ] c. presenting a persuasive argument.
- [ ] d. explaining a process.   _____

Vocabulary in Context   **6**   The word <u>straddles</u>, as used in the passage, means
- [ ] a. rides over.
- [ ] b. fights with.
- [ ] c. lies on both sides of.
- [ ] d. gets water from.   _____

Add your scores for questions 1–6. Enter the total here and on the graph on page 214.   **Total Score**   _____

96 An Unusual Reference Book

Where do you find out about the world's longest walk? The world's tallest man? The world's oldest woman? You know the answer, of course. It is the *Guinness Book of World Records.* How would people find such unusual facts without this book?

The Guinness Book did not exist until 1951. Here is what happened. The managing director of Guinness Brewery was a curious man. He wanted answers to some questions about records. For example, he wanted to know what was the fastest flying game bird in Europe. But he was frustrated. There was no book to answer questions like this.

The director, Sir Hugh Beaver, contacted the McWhirter twins. They were brothers who owned a research agency. He asked them to put together a new reference book. It would include all kinds of unusual records. The brothers quickly accepted. The first edition of their book was published in 1955. Soon the *Guinness Book of World Records* was a best seller. It has sold more copies than any book except the Bible. A new edition is published every year.

Where do all the book's records come from? They are a combination of things like natural wonders, sports records, and stunts. (How many people would push an egg with their noses if they weren't trying to get into the book?) But the editors try to keep things honest. All records must be <u>verified</u> by an investigator. Only then are they printed.

The Guinness Book is big business. It is published in dozens of languages. There are TV shows and museums. It is proof of how intrigued people are with strange pieces of information.

Main Idea	1		
		Answer	**Score**
	Mark the *main idea*	M	15
	Mark the statement that is *too broad*	B	5
	Mark the statement that is *too narrow*	N	5

a. Researchers named McWhirter were asked to compile the new reference book. ☐ _____

b. People like to read about unusual records. ☐ _____

c. The *Guinness Book of World Records* has been compiling unusual records since the 1950s. ☐ _____

Score 15 points for each correct answer.   Score

Subject Matter   **2**   This selection is mostly about
     ☐ a. the McWhirter twins.
     ☐ b. a history of the Guinness Book.
     ☐ c. unusual records in the Guinness Book.
     ☐ d. Sir Hugh Beaver.   _____

Supporting Details   **3**   The Guinness Book
     ☐ a. does not always check its records.
     ☐ b. is a best seller.
     ☐ c. is published only in English.
     ☐ d. has a full-length movie based on it.   _____

Conclusion   **4**   It is clear from the passage that the McWhirter twins
     ☐ a. recognized that Sir Hugh's idea for a book was a good one.
     ☐ b. liked to do everything together.
     ☐ c. were involved in politics.
     ☐ d. were responsible for building Guinness museums.   _____

Clarifying Devices   **5**   The sentence in parentheses in the fourth paragraph is
     ☐ a. a comparison.
     ☐ b. a story.
     ☐ c. one step in a process.
     ☐ d. an example.   _____

Vocabulary in Context   **6**   In this passage <u>verified</u> means
     ☐ a. questioned.
     ☐ b. written up.
     ☐ c. proved the truth of.
     ☐ d. blocked.   _____

Add your scores for questions 1–6. Enter the total here and on the graph on page 214.   Total Score   _____

97 The Oregon Trail

The United States was settled by people moving west. The eastern part of the country was settled fairly early. But in the mid-1800s, people were talking about going to far western regions. They heard about rich farmland along the West Coast. They heard about gold in California. Many wanted to start over, to build new lives. They wanted to be pioneers.

One trail in particular was <u>utilized</u> by these pioneers. It was the Oregon Trail. It began at Independence, Missouri. It ended in Fort Vancouver, Oregon. The distance was about 2,000 miles. Travel on this trail was hard. The first part of it crossed the dusty plains. Here the weather changed constantly. Then it climbed and crossed the Rockies through the steep, hard South Pass.

Most people traveled the trail by covered wagon. Inside the wagon were all their possessions. Women and children usually rode and slept in there. Wagons had canvas tops. These were soaked in oil. This made them rainproof. Usually oxen pulled the wagons. People brought these animals along to plow their new farms. But the oxen couldn't climb well. They had to be pushed up mountain passes. Often wagons got stuck in the mud. Then people would have to lighten the wagons. Sometimes this meant throwing out possessions. If there was no bridge across a river, the oxen had to haul the wagons across.

Along the trail were several forts. People could pick up some supplies at these, and repair broken wheels or axles. But food, water, and wood were usually hard to get.

Between 1845 and 1859, about 280,000 people used the Oregon Trail to go west.

Main Idea   1

	Answer	Score
Mark the *main idea*	M	15
Mark the statement that is *too broad*	B	5
Mark the statement that is *too narrow*	N	5

a. Traveling the Oregon Trail was a long, difficult ordeal. ☐ _____

b. People used the Oregon Trail to get to the West. ☐ _____

c. People carried some supplies, and picked up others on the trail. ☐ _____

Subject Matter **2** This passage is mostly about
☐ a. difficulties of traveling with oxen.
☐ b. going west on the Oregon Trail.
☐ c. the lands the Oregon Trail passed through.
☐ d. the kinds of possessions people took on the trail.   _____

Supporting Details **3** The Oregon Trail began
☐ a. in the Eastern United States.
☐ b. at Independence, Missouri.
☐ c. at Fort Vancouver.
☐ d. at South Pass.   _____

Conclusion **4** Pulling the wagons with oxen
☐ a. allowed the families to ride in the wagons.
☐ b. had certain disadvantages.
☐ c. made no sense.
☐ d. provided a food supply if necessary.   _____

Clarifying Devices **5** The author introduces the Oregon Trail by
☐ a. comparing it with other trails.
☐ b. talking about the wagons traveling on it.
☐ c. telling a story about a family on the trail.
☐ d. telling its distance and where it went.   _____

Vocabulary in Context **6** <u>Utilized</u> means
☐ a. built.
☐ b. carried.
☐ c. described.
☐ d. used.   _____

Add your scores for questions 1–6. Enter the total here   **Total**
and on the graph on page 214.   **Score**   _____

98 Booker T. Washington: Early Years

Tuskegee Institute. What is it? Where is it? If you said, "It is a historical black college in Alabama," you are correct. Is it as old as Yale, Harvard, or Princeton? No. It was founded in 1881. But its history is just as exciting. Harvard was founded by John Harvard. But who founded Tuskegee? The answer: Booker T. Washington.

Washington was born as a slave. The year was 1858 or 1859. After the slaves were freed, his family moved to West Virginia. As a child Washington had to work in a mine. But he met one African American there. This man read newspapers to the others. He inspired Washington to learn to read himself.

One man at the mine spoke about a college for blacks. Washington was thrilled. He found the full name. It was the Hampton Normal and Agricultural Institute. It was located in Virginia. The school was 500 miles away. Washington was <u>determined</u> to study there.

The Institute had been founded by the American Missionary Association. That group was founded in Boston by fighters against slavery. The teachers were from the North. Their goal was to train young African-American men and women. To train them as skilled craftsmen. To make good farmers of them. To teach women to be skilled homemakers. The plan was this. These trained African Americans would train other African Americans. Many at the school were ex-slaves. They needed help to do well in white society. This school would greatly influence Washington. It would help him when he set up Tuskegee.

Main Idea 1

	Answer	Score
Mark the *main idea*	M	15
Mark the statement that is *too broad*	B	5
Mark the statement that is *too narrow*	N	5

a. Booker T. Washington's early education prepared him to set up Tuskegee. ☐ _____

b. Tuskegee Institute was founded by Booker T. Washington. ☐ _____

c. Booker T. Washington attended the Hampton Normal and Agricultural Institute. ☐ _____

Subject Matter   **2**   This passage deals mostly with
- ☐ a. life on a plantation.
- ☐ b. trying to escape slavery.
- ☐ c. Booker T. Washington's early education.
- ☐ d. understanding what it takes to succeed.

_____

Supporting
Details   **3**   Booker T. Washington learned about reading by
- ☐ a. going to school.
- ☐ b. moving to West Virginia.
- ☐ c. listening to an African American read
  newspapers.
- ☐ d. working many jobs.

_____

Conclusion   **4**   From the last two sentences of the passage, we can
conclude that
- ☐ a. the Hampton Normal and Agricultural
  Institute impressed Washington.
- ☐ b. Washington wanted to stay at Hampton.
- ☐ c. Washington brought new students to
  Hampton.
- ☐ d. there were many schools like Hampton in
  the South.

_____

Clarifying
Devices   **5**   The author begins the passage with information
about Tuskegee Institute to
- ☐ a. explain what kind of school it is.
- ☐ b. compare it with Harvard.
- ☐ c. explain why Booker T. Washington went there.
- ☐ d. lead in to the Booker T. Washington story.

_____

Vocabulary
in Context   **6**   As used in the passage, <u>determined</u> means
- ☐ a. resolved.
- ☐ b. willing.
- ☐ c. happy.
- ☐ d. surprised.

_____

**Add your scores for questions 1–6. Enter the total here
and on the graph on page 214.**   **Total
Score**   _____

99 Setting Up Tuskegee

Booker T. Washington graduated from the Hampton Normal and Agricultural Institute. He gave the graduation address. He had learned many skills at Hampton. Among them, to lay bricks.

Three years later, a committee from Tuskegee wrote to Hampton. They asked for a white teacher for a normal school. The principal wrote back. He had no white teacher. But he had a talented African-American graduate. The committee wrote, "Send him at once."

Why was the school at Tuskegee founded? It was political. Colonel Foster, a white man, needed votes. Foster went to Lewis Adams, a black businessman. Adams made and sold shoes, harnesses, and tin articles. He made a deal with Foster. Foster must get money to support an African-American training school. And Adams would work to get him black votes.

The colonel agreed. The bargain was struck. Colonel Foster won his seat. The legislature acted. Some $2,000 would be provided annually for salaries. The normal school for African- American teachers would be in Tuskegee.

So Washington went to Tuskegee. And here is what he found. A small southern town with dusty roads. Half of the people were black. There was no school there. There was not even a building. And there was no land for a building. No students had been recruited. There was no money for land. No money for anything. The $2,000 was solely for salaries. The project looked hopeless. To Washington, it was a great challenge. He took a trip through the countryside. He saw how hard people's lives were. And he recruited 30 students. Half were women, half men.

Main Idea 1		
	Answer	**Score**
Mark the *main idea*	M	15
Mark the statement that is *too broad*	B	5
Mark the statement that is *too narrow*	N	5

a. Starting the school in Tuskegee was a challenge for Washington. ☐ ____

b. The school had money only for teachers' salaries. ☐ ____

c. Washington started the school in Tuskegee despite the problems he faced. ☐ ____

Subject Matter   **2** The topic of this passage is
                        ☐ a. Washington's education.
                        ☐ b. adventures in Washington's life.
                        ☐ c. the beginnings of the school in Tuskegee.
                        ☐ d. teachers who worked in Tuskegee.   _____

Supporting   **3** Lewis Adams
Details   ☐ a. asked Washington to teach at the school.
                        ☐ b. sold farm tools to whites.
                        ☐ c. was against slavery.
                        ☐ d. made a bargain with Colonel Foster.   _____

Conclusion   **4** When Washington arrived at Tuskegee, we can
                        conclude that he was
                        ☐ a. surprised.
                        ☐ b. amused.
                        ☐ c. angry.
                        ☐ d. ill.   _____

Clarifying   **5** To explain the founding of Tuskegee, the author uses
Devices   ☐ a. arguments.
                        ☐ b. a list of steps.
                        ☐ c. a story.
                        ☐ d. a discussion of the present school.   _____

Vocabulary   **6** The word <u>recruited</u> means
in Context   ☐ a. signed up.
                        ☐ b. accepted.
                        ☐ c. refused.
                        ☐ d. came.   _____

Add your scores for questions 1–6. Enter the total here   **Total**
and on the graph on page 214.   **Score**   _____

100 The Tuskegee Adventure

Booker T. Washington started Tuskegee with 30 students. But where were the school building and the classrooms? At the beginning, a church loaned Washington a dilapidated shanty. When it rained, a student held an umbrella over him as he lectured. It was discouraging. Almost everyone saw a failed enterprise. But Washington was too strong-willed to give up.

Then an abandoned plantation was put on sale. The house had burned, and the land was a jungle of weeds. There were, however, four buildings standing. One was a slaves' dining room. There were also an uncleaned hen house, a wooden kitchen, and a small stable. The owner asked $500 for the plantation. This included 100 acres of land in addition to the four buildings.

Washington was penniless, but he got a loan from the Hampton Institute. He closed the deal quickly and went right to work. After cleaning the filth, he moved the classes in the next day.

Washington had vision. He wanted brick buildings—permanence. There was good clay on the land. The students dug the clay and shaped it by hand into bricks. They also built a kiln.

Brickmaking was Tuskegee's first "practical skill." Businessmen now came to the campus to buy the bricks. Students who graduated with this skill got high pay. They were in demand throughout the state. Through bricks the fame of Tuskegee spread. More departments were created. Carpentry was added in 1884, printing in 1885. Cabinet-making came in 1887. When Washington died in 1915, the Institute had the following: over 100 well-equipped buildings, 1,500 students, and a faculty of 200. Washington had succeeded through sheer determination.

Main Idea 1

	Answer	Score
Mark the *main idea*	M	15
Mark the statement that is *too broad*	B	5
Mark the statement that is *too narrow*	N	5

a. Washington worked hard to improve the school and its classes. ☐ ____

b. Tuskegee gradually became a better place. ☐ ____

c. Washington wanted brick buildings for the school. ☐ ____

Score 15 points for each correct answer.

Subject Matter **2** This passage is mostly about
- ☐ a. Washington as a teacher.
- ☐ b. Tuskegee's buildings.
- ☐ c. Washington moving and growing the school.
- ☐ d. making brick buildings.

_____

Supporting Details **3** The school was moved to
- ☐ a. a new church.
- ☐ b. a jungle.
- ☐ c. an old plantation.
- ☐ d. a large stable.

_____

Conclusion **4** Readers are likely to admire Washington because he
- ☐ a. liked nice buildings.
- ☐ b. knew how to make bricks.
- ☐ c. did not hesitate to borrow money.
- ☐ d. never gave up.

_____

Clarifying Devices **5** The writer used the phrase "a dilapidated shanty," which suggests the structure was
- ☐ a. too big and all wood.
- ☐ b. free.
- ☐ c. very small and falling down.
- ☐ d. the worst school Tuskegee had.

_____

Vocabulary in Context **6** <u>Permanence</u> means a condition of
- ☐ a. order.
- ☐ b. lasting a long time.
- ☐ c. anger.
- ☐ d. being tall and strong.

_____

Add your scores for questions 1–6. Enter the total here and on the graph on page 214.

Total Score

_____

Diagnostic Chart (For Student Correction)

Directions: For each passage, write your answers to the left of the dotted line in the blocks for each skill category. Then correct your answers using the Answer Key. If your answer is correct, do not make any more marks in the block. If your answer is incorrect, write the letter of the correct answer to the right of the dotted line.

	Categories of Comprehension Skills							
	1 Main Idea				2	3	4	5	6
	Statement a	Statement b	Statement c	Subject Matter	Supporting Details	Conclusion	Clarifying Devices	Vocabulary in Context
Passage 1								
Passage 2								
Passage 3								
Passage 4								
Passage 5								
Passage 6								
Passage 7								
Passage 8								
Passage 9								
Passage 10								
Passage 11								
Passage 12								
Passage 13								
Passage 14								
Passage 15								
Passage 16								
Passage 17								
Passage 18								
Passage 19								
Passage 20								
Passage 21								
Passage 22								
Passage 23								
Passage 24								
Passage 25								

Diagnostic Chart: Passages 26–50

Directions: For each passage, write your answers to the left of the dotted line in the blocks for each skill category. Then correct your answers using the Answer Key. If your answer is correct, do not make any more marks in the block. If your answer is incorrect, write the letter of the correct answer to the right of the dotted line.

	Categories of Comprehension Skills								
	1 Main Idea			2	3	4	5	6	
	Statement a	Statement b	Statement c	Subject Matter	Supporting Details	Conclusion	Clarifying Devices	Vocabulary in Context	
Passage 26									
Passage 27									
Passage 28									
Passage 29									
Passage 30									
Passage 31									
Passage 32									
Passage 33									
Passage 34									
Passage 35									
Passage 36									
Passage 37									
Passage 38									
Passage 39									
Passage 40									
Passage 41									
Passage 42									
Passage 43									
Passage 44									
Passage 45									
Passage 46									
Passage 47									
Passage 48									
Passage 49									
Passage 50									

Diagnostic Chart: Passages 51–75

Directions: For each passage, write your answers to the left of the dotted line in the blocks for each skill category. Then correct your answers using the Answer Key. If your answer is correct, do not make any more marks in the block. If your answer is incorrect, write the letter of the correct answer to the right of the dotted line.

	Categories of Comprehension Skills								
	1 Main Idea			**2**	**3**		**4**	**5**	**6**
	Statement a	Statement b	Statement c	Subject Matter	Supporting Details	Conclusion	Clarifying Devices	Vocabulary in Context	
Passage 51									
Passage 52									
Passage 53									
Passage 54									
Passage 55									
Passage 56									
Passage 57									
Passage 58									
Passage 59									
Passage 60									
Passage 61									
Passage 62									
Passage 63									
Passage 64									
Passage 65									
Passage 66									
Passage 67									
Passage 68									
Passage 69									
Passage 70									
Passage 71									
Passage 72									
Passage 73									
Passage 74									
Passage 75									

Diagnostic Chart: Passages 76–100

Directions: For each passage, write your answers to the left of the dotted line in the blocks for each skill category. Then correct your answers using the Answer Key. If your answer is correct, do not make any more marks in the block. If your answer is incorrect, write the letter of the correct answer to the right of the dotted line.

	Categories of Comprehension Skills								
	1 Main Idea			2	3	4	5	6	
	Statement a	Statement b	Statement c	Subject Matter	Supporting Details	Conclusion	Clarifying Devices	Vocabulary in Context	
Passage 76									
Passage 77									
Passage 78									
Passage 79									
Passage 80									
Passage 81									
Passage 82									
Passage 83									
Passage 84									
Passage 85									
Passage 86									
Passage 87									
Passage 88									
Passage 89									
Passage 90									
Passage 91									
Passage 92									
Passage 93									
Passage 94									
Passage 95									
Passage 96									
Passage 97									
Passage 98									
Passage 99									
Passage 100									

Progress Graph

Directions: Write your Total Score for each passage in the comprehension score box under the number of the passage. Then plot your score on the graph itself by putting a small *x* on the line directly above the number of the passage, across from the score you got for that passage. As you mark your score for each passage, graph your progress by drawing a line to connect the *x*'s.

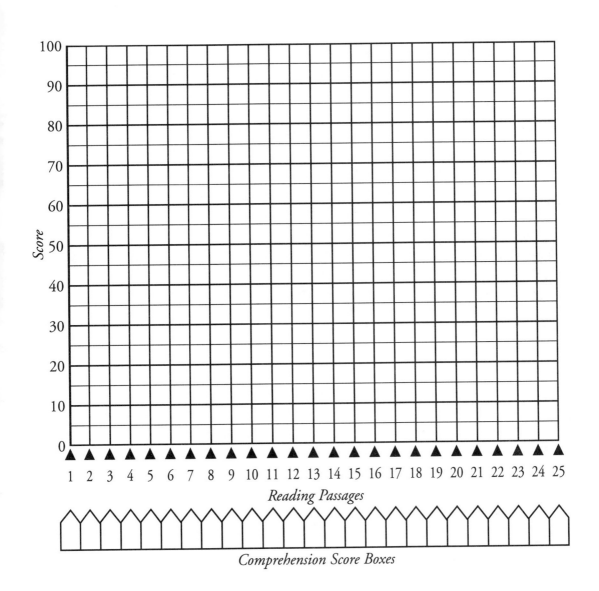

Reading Passages

Comprehension Score Boxes

Progress Graph: Passages 26–50

Directions: Write your Total Score for each passage in the comprehension score box under the number of the passage. Then plot your score on the graph itself by putting a small *x* on the line directly above the number of the passage, across from the score you got for that passage. As you mark your score for each passage, graph your progress by drawing a line to connect the *x*'s.

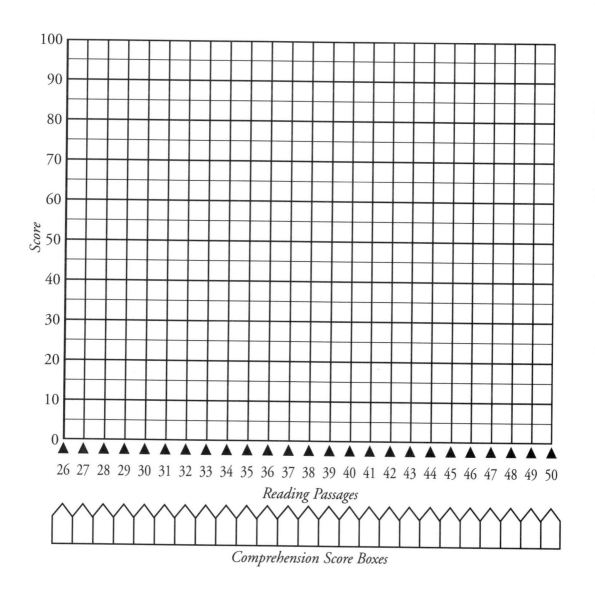

Reading Passages

Comprehension Score Boxes

Progress Graph: Passages 51–75

Directions: Write your Total Score for each passage in the comprehension score box under the number of the passage. Then plot your score on the graph itself by putting a small *x* on the line directly above the number of the passage, across from the score you got for that passage. As you mark your score for each passage, graph your progress by drawing a line to connect the *x*'s.

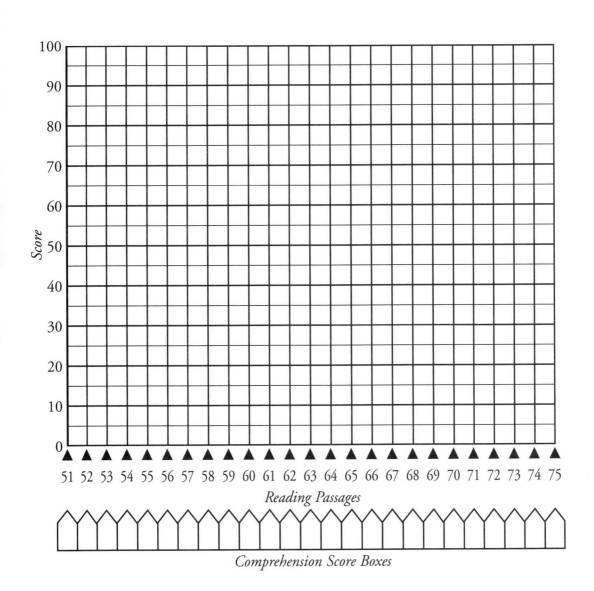

Reading Passages

Comprehension Score Boxes

Progress Graph: Passages 76–100

Directions: Write your Total Score for each passage in the comprehension score box under the number of the passage. Then plot your score on the graph itself by putting a small *x* on the line directly above the number of the passage, across from the score you got for that passage. As you mark your score for each passage, graph your progress by drawing a line to connect the *x*'s.

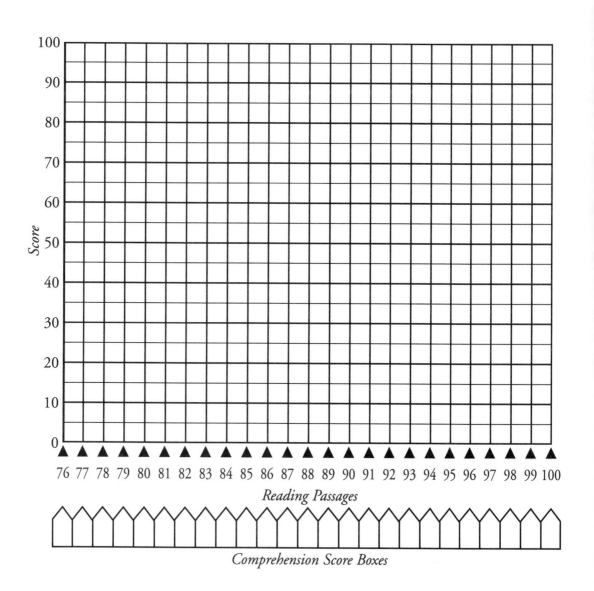